POWER FAITH

Balancing Faith
in
Words and Works

Roy H. Hicks, Jr.

with

Jack W. Hayford

THOMAS NELSON PUBLISHERS
Nashville • Atlanta • London • Vancouver

DEDICATION

This, the third series of *Spirit-Filled Life
Bible Study Guides,* is dedicated to the
memory of

Dr. Roy H. Hicks, Jr.
(1944–1994)

one of God's "men for all seasons,"
faithful in the Word, mighty in the Spirit,
leading multitudes into the love of God
and the worship of His Son, Jesus Christ.

Unto Christ's glory and in Roy's memory,
we will continue to sing:

Praise the Name of Jesus,
Praise the Name of Jesus,
He's my Rock, He's my Fortress,
He's my Deliverer, in Him will I trust.
Praise the Name of Jesus.

Words by Roy Hicks, Jr., © 1976 Latter Rain Music. All rights administered by
The Sparrow Corp. All Rights Reserved. Used by Permission.

**Power Faith: Balancing Faith in
Words and Works**
Copyright © 1994 by Jack W. Hayford

Published in Nashville, Tennessee, by Thomas Nelson, Inc.

Unless otherwise indicated, Scripture quotations are from the
New King James Version of the Bible, © 1979, 1980, 1982,
Thomas Nelson, Inc., Publishers

Printed in the United States of America
8 — 00 99 98 97

CONTENTS

Power Faith: Balancing Faith in Words and Works is one of a series of study guides that focus exciting, discovery-geared coverage of Bible book and power themes—all prompting toward dynamic, Holy Spirit-filled living.

About the Author

ROY HICKS, JR., went to his eternal reward only on short month after he had completed this manuscript study on faith. As a man who uniquely demonstrated a vital, victorious commitment to Holy Spirit-filled ministry, he not only moved in a precious dimension of divine grace, but he wooed others to do the same.

He graduated from LIFE Bible College in 1966, and for the years immediately following led his denomination's youth in the Northwest District of the Foursquare Church. Then, in 1969 he accepted the pastorate of the Eugene, Oregon, church, soon to be known as Faith Center. From this scene of divine visitation, where growth took the body from a handful to thousands over ensuing years, a virtual plethora of ministries broke forth over the region and across the nation, as well as in other countries. Roy's last years of ministry were served as International Director of Missions for the Church of the Foursquare Gospel—a position he filled until 1993. He concluded his earthly journey as his private plane malfunctioned during a storm in February 1994. He was returning to Eugene from Southern California where he had been involved in ministry. He was fifty years old.

Roy's wife, Kay Hicks, continues to live in Eugene with her and Roy's teen-aged son, Jeff; both surrounded by the love of the congregation they served for nearly twenty years.

Of this contributor, the Executive Editor has remarked: "I've never known a more intense servant of Jesus who at the same time retained a warm sense of humanity. Roy could mix fun and faith without confusing the two, and always sought to live on the cutting edge of the precise thing the Holy Spirit wanted to do in every situation. His passing is an immeasurable loss. A giant has fallen from our midst."

About the Executive Editor

JACK W. HAYFORD, noted pastor, teacher, writer, and composer, is the Executive Editor of the complete series, working with the publisher in the conceiving and developing of each of the books.

Dr. Hayford is Senior Pastor of The Church On The Way, the First Foursquare Church of Van Nuys, California. He and his wife, Anna, have four married children, all of whom are active in either pastoral ministry or vital church life. As Executive Editor of the Spirit-Filled Life Bible, Pastor Hayford led a four-year project, which has resulted in the availability of one of today's most practical and popular study Bibles. He is author of more than twenty books, including *A Passion for Fullness, The Beauty of Spiritual Language, Rebuilding the Real You*, and *Prayer Is Invading the Impossible*. His musical compositions number over four hundred songs, including the widely sung "Majesty."

THE KEYS
THAT KEEP ON FREEING

Is there anything that holds more mystery or more genuine practicality than a key? The mystery: "What does it fit?
What can it turn on? What might it open? What new discovery
could be made? The practicality: Something *will* most certainly
open to the possessor! Something *will* absolutely be found to
unlock and allow a possibility otherwise obstructed!

- Keys describe the instruments we use to access or
  ignite.
- Keys describe the concepts that unleash mind-bog-
  gling possibilities.
- Keys describe the different structures of musical
  notes which allow variation and range.

Jesus spoke of keys: "And I will give you the keys of the
kingdom of heaven, and whatever you bind on earth will be
bound in heaven, and whatever you loose on earth will be
loosed in heaven" (Matt. 16:19).

While there is no conclusive list of exactly what keys Jesus
was referring to, it is clear that He did confer upon His
church—upon *all* who believe—the access to a realm of spiritual partnership with Him in the dominion of His kingdom.
Faithful students of the Word of God, moving in the practical
grace and biblical wisdom of Holy Spirit-filled living and ministry, have noted some of the primary themes which undergird
this order of "spiritual partnership" Christ offers. The "keys"
are *concepts*—biblical themes that are traceable through the
Scriptures and verifiably dynamic when applied with soundly
based faith under the lordship of Jesus Christ. The "partnership" is the *essential* feature of this release of divine grace;

(1) believers reaching to *receive* Christ's promise of "kingdom keys," (2) while choosing to *believe* in the Holy Spirit's readiness to actuate their unleashing, unlimited power today.

Companioned with the Bible book studies in the *Spirit-Filled Life Study Guide* series, the Kingdom Dynamic studies present a dozen different themes. This study series is an outgrowth of the Kingdom Dynamics themes included throughout the *Spirit-Filled Life Bible,* which provide a treasury of insight developed by some of today's most respected Christian leaders. From that beginning, studious writers have evolved the elaborated studies you'll pursue here.

The central goal of the subjects focused on in this present series of study guides is to relate "power points" of the Holy Spirit-filled life. Assisting you in your discoveries are a number of helpful features. Each study guide has twelve to fourteen lessons, each arranged so you can plumb the depths or skim the surface, depending upon your needs and interests. The study guides contain major lesson features, each marked by a symbol and heading for easy identification.

WORD WEALTH

The WORD WEALTH feature provides important definitions of key terms.

BEHIND THE SCENES

BEHIND THE SCENES supplies information about cultural beliefs and practices, doctrinal disputes, business trades, and the like, that illuminate Bible passages and teachings.

AT A GLANCE

The AT A GLANCE feature uses maps and charts to identify places and simplify themes or positions.

 ## KINGDOM EXTRA

Because this study guide focuses on a theme of the Bible, you will find a KINGDOM EXTRA feature that guides you into Bible dictionaries, Bible encyclopedias, and other resources that will enable you to glean more from the Bible's wealth on the topic if you want something extra.

 ## PROBING THE DEPTHS

Another feature, PROBING THE DEPTHS, will explain controversial issues raised by particular lessons and cite Bible passages and other sources to which you can turn to help you come to your own conclusions.

 ## FAITH ALIVE

Finally, each lesson contains a FAITH ALIVE feature. Here the focus is, So what? Given what the Bible says, what does it mean for my life? How can it impact my day-to-day needs, hurts, relationships, concerns, and whatever else is important to me? FAITH ALIVE will help you see and apply the practical relevance of God's literary gift.

As you'll see, these guides supply space for you to answer the study and life-application questions and exercises. You may, however, want to record all your answers, or just the overflow from your study or application, in a separate notebook or journal. This would be especially helpful if you think you'll dig into the KINGDOM EXTRA features. Because the exercises in this feature are optional and can be expanded as far as you want to take them, we have not allowed writing space for them in this study guide. So you may want to have a notebook or journal handy for recording your discoveries while working through to this feature's riches.

The Bible study method used in this series revolves around four basic steps: observation, interpretation, correlation, and application. Observation answers the question, What does the text say? Interpretation deals with, What does the text mean? —not with what it means to you or me, but what it meant to its original readers. Correlation asks, What light do other Scripture passages shed on this text? And application, the goal of Bible study, poses the question, How should my life change in response to the Holy Spirit's teaching of this text?

If you have used a Bible much before, you know that it comes in a variety of translations and paraphrases. Although you can use any of them with profit as you work through the *Spirit-Filled Life Kingdom Dynamics Study Guide* series, when Bible passages or words are cited, you will find they are from the New King James Version of the Bible. Using this translation with this series will make your study easier, but it's certainly not necessary.

The only resources you need to complete and apply these study guides are a heart and mind open to the Holy Spirit, a prayerful attitude, and a pencil and a Bible. Of course, you may draw upon other sources, such as commentaries, dictionaries, encyclopedias, atlases, and concordances, and you'll even find some optional exercises that will guide you into these sources. But these are extras, not necessities. These study guides are comprehensive enough to give you all you need to gain a good, basic understanding of the Bible book being covered and how you can apply its themes and counsel to your life.

A word of warning, though. By itself, Bible study will not transform your life. It will not give you power, peace, joy, comfort, hope, and a number of other gifts God longs for you to unwrap and enjoy. Through Bible study, you will grow in your understanding of the Lord, His kingdom and your place in it, and those things are essential. But you need more. You need to rely on the Holy Spirit to guide your study and your application of the Bible's truths. He, Jesus promised, was sent to teach us "all things" (John 14:26; cf. 1 Cor. 2:13). So as you use this series to guide you through Scripture, bathe your study time in prayer, asking the Spirit of God to illuminate the text, enlighten your mind, humble your will, and comfort your heart. He will never let you down.

My prayer and goal for you is that as you unlock and begin to explore God's Book for living His way, the Holy Spirit will fill every fiber of your being with the joy and power God longs to give all His children. So read on. Be diligent. Stay open and submissive to Him. You will not be disappointed. He promises you!

Introduction:
A Balanced View

Every believer knows what it means to struggle with faith. Am I trusting God enough? Would she have been healed if only I had trusted God more? Did I fail to get that promotion because I lacked faith? If I am really trusting God, why am I still having these unforgiving thoughts? If my faith is strong, why are my children having so many problems? If I moved with faith, wouldn't the people to whom I witness always accept Christ as their Savior?

Perhaps the Apostle Paul was referring to this conflict when he used the phrase, "the good fight of faith" (1 Tim 6:12). For him, faith's struggle was not merely in matters of ministry. Though the pioneering of churches throughout Asia must have involved many conflicts in faith, Paul's "good fight" was referring more to the whole of his relationship with the Lord Jesus. Writing at the end of his life, and from a jail cell, aware that he could be summoned at any moment to his execution, Paul admits that faith has been a fight, albeit a *good* one.

It may be a gigantic step for you even to come to the place of accepting that there is such a thing as a "good fight." This present culture doesn't believe in fighting for too many things. But if there ever was something worth fighting for, faith is it.

Why is faith worth fighting for? Why is the fight for faith a good fight?

Because:
- *Anything done without faith cannot please God (Heb. 11:6).*
- *Grace can be accessed only by faith (Eph. 2:8).*
- *Every person has the capacity for faith (Rom. 12:3).*
- *Faith is one of the gifts of the Holy Spirit (1 Cor. 12:7–11).*

- *Nothing is impossible when you have faith, even though it may be as small as a mustard seed (Matt. 17:14-21).*

The fight of faith is a good fight.

The Bible is clear in its teaching concerning the power of faith. However, many believers are confused concerning matters of faith. This confusion exists in part because of the variety of high-profile "faith" ministries. Some minister effectively, while others appear to use faith in such a way that makes man the master of his own destiny, rather than God the Sovereign Lord.

But even if there were no provocative teachers and teachings, there would still be a struggle in the arena of faith. Why? Because, at the risk of oversimplification, faith has an enemy. Actually, your faith has *two* enemies. One of them is you. The other is Satan.

Satan has many devices he employs in his attack on your life. But it may surprise you to discover that the focus of his attack is directed almost exclusively towards your faith. He well knows if he can make your faith ineffective, you will be ineffective. He wants to overthrow your faith (read 2 Tim. 2:18).

Not all of your struggle with faith will be caused by Satan. Some of it will be caused by your own "natural man" (see 1 Cor. 2:14). Faith involves hearing, making choices, repenting, and learning. All of these are challenging without the devil's interference. Since the devil knows just how difficult this "good fight of faith" can be, he seeks to influence you by his lies.

We can be deceived, and because Satan is cunning, our intake of God's Word becomes crucial in cultivating, growing, and evaluating our faith. It is through His Word that faith is made alive (Rom. 10:17). And it is with His Word that we fight against the enemy (Eph. 6:17).

During this study in God's Word, you will consider many important faith questions.

- Can I ask God for anything, and as long as I have the right faith, get what I ask for?
- If I believe, can I have assurance that my children will be saved?
- Does faith guarantee that I will never have to deal with sickness or pain?

• Is there ever a time when my lack of faith might make God angry? If I make Him mad, am I still saved?

Coming to the "full assurance of faith" is worth fighting the good fight of faith. Let's find faith's *way* according to God's *Word*!

Lesson 1/The History of Faith

Someone has recently noted that our world desperately needs heroes. In matters of faith, they are in abundance. Every church age has its own hall of heroes who are rightly honored. However, the most moving account of faith heroes is given in Hebrews 11. As we begin our study of the history of faith, pause here and read completely through the entire chapter of Hebrews 11, finishing with Hebrews 12:1–2. Exciting reading, isn't it? Doesn't it make your heart quicken a beat?

Did you notice that both those who experienced great victory, as well as those who lived in faith without *ever* experiencing a victory, are listed together? Read 11:33–34 again. What did faith enable them to do?

Now, read again from the second sentence in 11:35–38. What did faith enable these heroes to do?

 WORD WEALTH

1 John 5:4 ". . . And this is the victory that has overcome the world—our faith." A sensible "faith" question is, When do you win? When are you victorious? Our society suggests that the experience of victory can only be real when you have *what* you want *when* you want it. But the Bible teaches that you win, not when you get what you want, but *the moment you believe!* If I'm surrounded by problems, I win *not* when they're solved, but the moment I believe God's bound that He'll sustain me through or beyond it. If I am sick, I win over sickness; not when I get well, but the moment I believe in

God's promises which make Jesus Christ the Healer alive and real to me. If I find myself in poverty, I win the moment I believe what He has said about my financial circumstances. You and I are overcomers the moment we place our faith in the Son of God, and what His Word is speaking into our lives.

Here in 1 John 5:4, the word "overcome" is used twice, and victory, once. Each usage comes from the same Greek word, *nike* (*Strong's #3528, 3529*; *neeh*-kay). It looks like the name of a popular athletic shoe manufacturer, doesn't it? This is, of course, because they chose the name for their company from this Greek word since it is also the name of the goddess of victory in Greek mythology. But military or athletic victory, that which the Greeks referred to, which focuses only on human goals, is only that—a myth. What is real and what has substance is this: When you put your faith in the Son of God—when you become one born of God—your faith then makes you an overcomer and gives you a victory that can never be taken away from you!

HEROES OF FAITH

Please use your Bible to answer the following questions about the heroes of faith mentioned in Hebrews 11. As you answer the questions, you'll also be considering the principles for effective, practical faith that are on display there.

Who is the faith hero first mentioned in this chapter? And what does he do in faith? (v. 4)

What happened to Enoch? How did he please God? (v. 5)

PROBING THE DEPTHS

Faith that pleases God does these three things according to Hebrews 11:6:

• *Pleasing faith comes actively before God*—"those who diligently seek Him." To be diligent, as it is used here, means to investigate, crave, or demand. It is an insistent coming. Nothing in this graphic word picture is intended to portray someone nagging God! However, Jesus Himself taught two parables lauding this diligent, aggressive seeking attitude in prayer. Read one of them in Luke 11:5–10. The Lord doesn't want you to think He's asleep, or uncaring about your predicament. However, He does want you to come before Him unashamedly insistent! The oft-heard word "importunity" ("insistence" in v. 8) comes from two Greek words, meaning "without bashfulness."

Write your thoughts on this parable, noting Jesus' desire to instill boldness in asking (as contrasted with mere *tenacity*). Look up the words and discern this important truth.

- *Pleasing faith believes God exists*—"believe[s] that He is." Some people's prayers sound as though they were talking to themselves! Have you ever prayed without even thinking of standing in His presence? God wants your faith to focus on the reality of His being. Contrary to modern world views, God *is* there!—and He insists that you think so in order to please Him.

   For most of us this is theoretically not an issue. As a Christian, you have already professed faith in God through Christ. In that sense, you believe He exists. The problem comes when we're under pressure. Do we believe He exists in these troubling circumstances? That's when your faith pleases God—when by faith you can see Him *in* your situation.

- *Pleasing faith believes God is a rewarder*—"and that He is a rewarder." In some cultures, this word might simply mean a good employer. It has the sense of wages, money given for hire. If it were only to mean that, then God is pleased when you believe He's a good boss! But it's much more than believing God gives good wages. "Rewarder" has the meaning of beyond recompense, of reimbursing beyond the value of what was received. Isn't that exactly what Ephesians 3:20–21 is saying? Approach it from the negative point of inquiry. How can I please God when I believe He rewards less than I am asking? Biblical answer: God can't be pleased when we believe He only-but-slightly answers prayer with "just enough" to get us through our circumstance. Remember: Pleasing faith believes God rewards beyond normal recompense when He is diligently sought.

MORE HEROES OF FAITH

What did Noah do by faith? (v. 7)

Having condemned the attitude of the world in which Noah lived, what did he become?

Read Ephesians 5:1–11, to see how your walk of faith does today what Noah's life of faith did in his day.

Though Abraham's life of faith is studied elsewhere in these lessons, read Hebrews 11:8–12, 17. Write out your thoughts on each of these statements.

- By faith Abraham obeyed (v. 8).

- By faith Abraham went out—clearly directed, yet with unclear directions (v. 8).

- By faith Abraham dwelt in a Promised Land but as a stranger—God promised him the land but he never got to live in it as his own (v. 9).

- By faith Abraham waited—he saw an eternal city made by God (v. 10).

• By faith Sarah received strength for child-bearing in her old age (v. 11).

• By faith Abraham offered up Isaac, believing that God was able to raise Isaac from the dead if necessary since his birth was like a resurrection miracle (v. 17).

In Hebrews 11:13–16, a remarkable litany of faith is recited. If you memorize this rhythmic statement of faith, your personal faith life will be greatly enhanced. Now note five more characteristics of faith these verses reveal:

1. *Faith is assured.* Paul uses this word when he says he has become persuaded that nothing can separate the believer from God's love in Christ (Rom. 8:38). It always involves a process of thought; persuasion requires process, time. He uses the same word again to speak of the confidence he has in Christ finishing the good work He has begun in every believer (Phil. 1:6).

   Perhaps the most moving usage of this word occurs when Paul writes to Timothy who has begun to battle fear while pastoring in Ephesus. As a loving father, he invites Timothy to take his place in the work of faith, saying, "I am not ashamed, for I know whom I have believed, and am *persuaded* that He is able to keep what I have committed to Him until that Day." The Greek is *peitho* (*Strong's #3982*). It has the meaning of having experienced a debate in which all the relevant ideas have been given a fair hearing. When all the issues have been considered, a decision is made, based on all the evidence and an inner conviction. When this has happened, you are persuaded.

   How is faith persuaded? This persuasion comes by considering all that God's Word has to say on the issues being considered, and by exposure to the person of the Word, the

Lord Jesus. The combination of the written Word and the revealed Word in the person of Jesus Christ accomplishes this glorious persuasion. The question is: What "words" of promise form the basis for your current persuasion?

2. *Faith embraces.* This word (*aspadzomai, Strong's #782;* oss-*pod*-zuh-my) is most often used in the beginning of the epistles when the writer "greets" the church. Sometimes the apostle will instruct the believers to greet one another—this is that word. It can mean to enfold someone in your arms, to salute (greet), or to welcome. As the assurance of faith involves considering the promises and becoming persuaded by them, so "embracing" means to take them in! Now that you see them for what they are, greet them, hug them, hold them, welcome them into your life. As you would embrace a loved one, so you are to treat the promises God has spoken into your life. Make them your friends. In several usages, it even has the connotation of great affection, being translated "to kiss." The question is: What biblical "words" of faith have you taken into your life as friends?

3. *Faith confesses.* The Greek word *homologeo* (*Strong's #3670;* hahm-ahl-ahg-*eh*-oh) means to give assent, covenant, or to acknowledge. A contractual meaning is suggested, as when a building project is to begin. Jesus uses this word when He says, "Whoever confesses Me before men, . . . [I] also will confess . . ." (Luke 12:8). It means "to speak the same thing." Faith aligns the persuading word with the embraced word to the spoken word. What should you be confessing in your present circumstance? You should be confessing what you have become persuaded of—you should be confessing what you are welcoming into your life. Put it in the negative: What should you not be confessing? You should not confess things of which you are not persuaded. You should not be confessing things you are, in fact, not welcoming into your life.

    Jesus said, "Out of the abundance of the heart, the mouth speaks" (Matt. 12:34). My friend and pastor, Steve Overman, says often, "The Word of God will always tell you what's going on in God's heart. Unfortunately, *your* words will always tell you what's going on in *your* heart!" The question is: What is the condition of your heart towards the promises of God as indicated by your confession?

4. *Faith declares plainly.* Why is this different from what we just studied? The preceding has to do with vocabulary—the words you have been using that tell the condition of your heart towards the promises of God. This present declaration comes more as a manifestation of a life decision that you have made which is evident to all. The Greek word for manifest, *emphanidzo* (*Strong's #1718;* em-fan-*id*-zoh), is used to describe the manifestation of the life, what others can plainly see because of life-style and conversation. Jesus uses this word when speaking of the spiritual manifestation He and the Father will make to every believer when the Holy Spirit is received (John 14:21). The combination of words used here in Hebrews suggests clarity. There can be no disputing of what is being declared. It is obvious. The "plainly declaring" phrase may certainly involve language, but it is much more than that. If you are around someone who is "declaring plainly" (as the word is used here), you will hear what is being spoken through body language, decisions, actions, and their words. Their life "plainly declares." And in this instance, the lives of these believers "plainly declared" that they had become persuaded of God's promise, that they had welcomed God's promise into their lives, that they were speaking what God what was promising, and that their entire life-style proved that this faith was real. The question is: What is your life telling about your faith to the people who know you best?

5. *Faith calls to mind.* Almost every time this word is used, it's translated "to remember." It carries the idea of controlling your thought life; being in charge of what you are thinking. It also implies controlling what you are thinking by speaking of the thing you wish to remember.

The apostle writing this letter teaches all who are serious about their faith a remarkable lesson: If you place in your mind an objective other than the one outlined in God's promise, you'll have an opportunity to reach that objective! Amazing, isn't it?

If the pilgrims of Hebrews 13:13 had focused on the country they left behind to follow God's call, numerous opportunities to go back would have appeared. Instead, however, they focused on the land of God's promise, a better, heavenly country. They "called to mind" a goal that rested in the center of God's promises.

The important thing to remember is that we are to be absolutely in control of what we think. Some may argue that we can overdo this. Yet God would not give instructions on how to think (see Phil. 4:8) if it were not possible to do exactly what He has said!

Write Jesus' words in Luke 21:19.

Now, rewrite them, noting that to "possess" means "to acquire control of," and that your "soul" includes your *mind* and *feelings*.

One practice of the life of faith is to memorize God's Word. Repeat the promises. Call them to mind. *Focus* on them. If you are struggling at all with your thought life, what does the psalmist say in Psalm 119:11?

The question confronting us is: What have we been calling to mind?

6. *Faith desires.* The Greek word *oregamai* (*Strong's #3713;* or-*eg*-om-ï) signifies an inner choice to reach for something, to stretch oneself out to an extreme position of vulnerability, as in saying, "This is what I want to do with my life." It's the word used in 1 Timothy when Paul says that it's a good thing to *desire* the office of a bishop. In its negative form, it's also the word used to describe someone coveting an object not yet possessed. In the positive, you would use this word in the phrase, "This is the desire of my life." Faith desires the fulfillment of what God has promised. The question is: What is the desire of your life?

This faith litany, if you will commit it to memory, can become a gridwork for evaluating your faith life. Have you caught the contradiction? At least, some think it is a contradiction to understanding the life of faith. We have been discussing the faith life of those who never received what they were believing for! Does this bother you?

It will not bother you if you understand the practical purpose of our faith life is to bring us where God wants us to go. It is not a tool for self-accomplishment, but for God's accomplishing His purpose in us as we actively, aggressively open up to His Word, will, promise, and power.

Read Hebrews 11:16. These are the very people of whom God "is not ashamed to be called their God." The obvious thought is that, sometimes, God is ashamed! When is that? Whenever our faith is an attempt to appropriate the goodness of God for this life only, forgetting that His plan is an eternal one! Write a statement of your own: "Lord, I want to have You rejoice over my faith!"

Yet More Heroes of Faith

Write out your thoughts on how the faith of Isaac, Jacob, and Joseph is mentioned (Heb. 11:20–22). Doesn't the life of faith plan on generational succession? How is it true that a person of faith has something to say upon his or her passing?

What did Moses choose in faith? What did Moses esteem?

Read Hebrews 11:33, 34. Note the exploits of those motivated by faith. They—

Subdued kingdoms.
Worked righteousness.
Obtained promises.
Stopped the mouths of lions.
Quenched the violence of fire.
Escaped the edge of the sword.
Were made strong out of weakness.
Became valiant in battle.
Turned to flight the armies of the aliens.

 FAITH ALIVE

Since "faith is the substance of things hoped for, the evidence of things not seen," write out some of the things you are hoping for but do not yet see. As you do, let the Holy Spirit remind you of God's Word. Write those promises alongside the things you're hoping for, but not yet seeing.

Lesson 2/The Gift of Faith

The elevator was too slow. So, I took the stairs. Two steps at a time, I climbed the three flights of stairs as fast as I could move. They had called while he was en route to the hospital. Short, terse words were spoken. Before I could ask any questions, the line went dead. Yet, I was smiling as I climbed the stairs.

Why? It wasn't that Hank was too young to die of heart failure. I knew better than that. A heart attack can happen to anyone, at any age. It wasn't that he was a strong believer who knew how to lay claim to the provisions of healing grace. Hardly. Hank was a believer, but a young one. I knew him pretty well. Hank would struggle to locate the Gospel of John, let alone any passages on healing!

But I was smiling. Why? I was smiling because I knew that Hank was going to be OK. This knowledge didn't come from the terse words that had summoned me to the hospital. My smile wasn't caused by medical knowledge—or, by a lack of it. I was smiling because I recognized the *gift of faith*.

This was not the first time. It had happened before, once when I had knelt beside a nine-year-old girl who had just been struck by a truck. I had been driving the car behind the truck that had hit her. As I knelt beside her, it was apparent that she had sustained serious injury. The head was misshapen from the blow. Blood was coming from her ear. I could hear the mother screaming in the background and people yelling for someone to call an ambulance.

Knowing that she should not be moved, I began to whisper in her ear. "You're going to be all right. The Lord is going to take care of you. You will live, and be completely restored," I quietly spoke to her. It was true! I was not just attempting to comfort her with words of confidence. I somehow knew that she would completely recover.

I was experiencing a *gift of faith*.

And she did recover. So did Hank. I wish it happened all the time, but it doesn't. Even people with the strongest of faith admit that the *gift of faith*, while not rare, is not the common experience. The common experience in faith is a matter of choice. The believer chooses to believe what God has said in His Word. And the next chapter in this study guide is devoted to exploring that expression of faith we'll call *the choice of faith*. But now we're looking at this other work of God's Spirit, when faith functions as a "gift" because *He*—the Holy Spirit—has simply *given it* into a situation where you, I, or another Christian "happens" to be the instrument He has chosen to use in ministering this "gift." It's that gift referred to in 1 Corinthians 12:9, "to another faith by the same Spirit. . . ."

Turn to 1 Corinthians 12:7–11 and examine it to answer these questions:

1. To whom is the manifestation of the Spirit given and why?

2. Write down the nine manifestations of spiritual gifts listed in this passage.

3. Who works all these different gifts, and by whose will do they work?

 WORD WEALTH

Faith, *pistis* (*Strong's #4102*). The word means persuasion, i.e. credence; moral conviction of religious truth, or the truthfulness of God. It carries the connotation of assurance, belief, believe, faith, fidelity.

WORD WEALTH

Gift, *charisma* (*Strong's #5486*). A (divine) gratuity, i.e. deliverance (from danger or passion); a spiritual endowment or miraculous faculty; a free gift.

Putting these two words together, "faith" and "gift," then adding the thought that this *charisma* of faith comes from the working of the Holy Spirit, the stage is set for some remarkable possibilities!

THE APOSTLE PAUL

The Apostle Paul experienced the gift of faith many times. We can read about one such time in Acts 27:6–44. Read how this passage describes Paul's journey to Rome as a captive. See how, even though Paul warned the captain of the ship, he still set sail at the most dangerous time of the year. (See map on page 26.)

With your Bible open at this account, answer the following questions:

1. What did Paul first say about loss of life? (Acts 27:10)

2. What did Paul say about loss of life after the storm had begun? (Acts 27:22)

3. On what basis did Paul make this promise? (Acts 27:23–24)

4. What did Paul believe? (Acts 27:25)

Paul's unswerving confidence in this situation was not by strength of a powerful human "will" to believe. It was due to a visition of the Lord "giving" *faith* at an otherwise seemingly impossible juncture. When we study it objectively, the *gift of faith* appears to function without external stimulus. By that I mean, the attending circumstances are dictating, or at least

AT A GLANCE

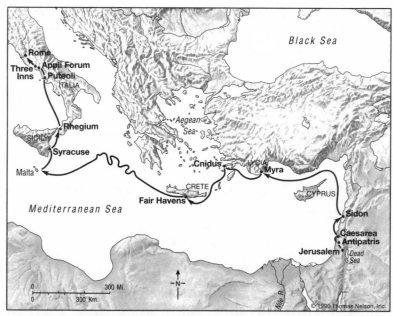

On to Rome (Paul's Fourth Journey, Acts 27:1—28:16). In Jerusalem following his third missionary journey, Paul struggled with Jews who accused him of profaning the temple (Acts 21:26–34). He was placed in Roman custody in Caesarea for two years, but after appealing to Caesar, was sent by ship to Rome. After departing the island of Crete, Paul's party was shipwrecked on Malta by a great storm. Three months later he finally arrived at the imperial city.[1]

suggesting, something else. For example, the storm did not suggest everything would be all right! Rather, Paul's faith came from something internal, not external. It was supernatural, not natural. And it was based on what Paul understood the Lord to be saying, rather than anything being spoken by earthly authority or generated by human will or religious zeal.

CALEB

In the Old Testament, there are similar accounts of supernatural faith. One of them is the story of the twelve spies, sent by Moses into Canaan. They were to bring back a report to Israel. Ten of the spies brought back a humanly realistic, militarily practical, and completely negative report. In contrast, two of the spies gave a positive report which seemed to miss the actual challenges being faced.

From the account of this incident in Numbers 13:17–33, answer these questions:

1. What was the assignment given to the spies?

2. How long were the spies gone?

3. What did Caleb say?

  WORD WEALTH

We are more than **able**—*yakol* (*Strong's* #3201; *yawkole*): To be able; to have power; having the capacity to prevail or succeed. This verb is used 200 times in the Old Testament. Generally, it is translated by such English words as "can," "could," or "be able"; in a few references, "prevail"

(1 Ki. 22:22; Esth. 6:13); sometimes, "to have power." In Esther 8:6, it is translated as "endure": the compassionate queen asks, "How can I endure to see the evil that will come to my people?" Here in Numbers 13, Caleb uses the intensive repetition of *yakol:* "Let us go up . . . we are well able to overcome it"[2]

As you've studied these verses, you have noticed the contrast between what Caleb reports and the advice of the other ten spies! It is obvious that Caleb is speaking with amazing faith. Where does this faith come from? How can Caleb speak with such confidence when the other men are saying just the opposite?

For the answer, read Numbers 14:24. What kind of "spirit" does Caleb have?

"Spirit" refers to Caleb's inner man, not the person of the Holy Spirit. But it is still a reference to help us see how the gift of faith can function within us.

Caleb was not moved by the giants he saw during his forty days of spying. He was not awed by the walled cities or the enormous size of the land. Instead, because Caleb "followed [the Lord] fully," he not only saw the giants, he could also see the Lord! Even though he saw the walled cities, he could also see the Lord. Caleb saw the largeness of the land, but he also saw the Lord. People who fully follow the Lord are able to see the Lord in their circumstances. They are not ignorant of the challenges, not playing "mind games," pretending to deny the reality of what is being faced—but they are seeing the Lord above and beyond the problems!

The gift of faith, that supernatural working of the Holy Spirit, comes to those being filled with that Spirit. Like all the other gifts, the gift of faith flows to those who are allowing the Holy Spirit to work in them. Caleb's confession of faith speaks of his character and his choice to believe. Yet, as with Paul on board the ship, when all the circumstance is examined, no external influence can be found which would justify Caleb's confession. The giants in the land, the size of the land, the walled cities of the land all would suggest a report best summed up in the words of the other spies!

But Caleb's report is different, not just because of his character, not just because of his choice—but because he is being influenced by the Spirit of God. It is a supernatural faith that says, "We are well able to overcome!"

 ## BEHIND THE SCENES

My father, Dr. Roy Hicks, Sr., says of Caleb's confession, "Caleb saw the same giants and walled city as the other spies, but the ten spies brought back an 'evil report' of unbelief. Caleb's words declared a conviction—a "confession"—before all Israel: "We are well able to overcome." He had surveyed the land, a reminder that faith is not blind. Faith does not deny the reality of difficulty; it declares the power of God in the face of the problem.

There is a message in the spirit of Caleb's response to those who rejected his faith-filled report. While today some people use their "confession" of faith to cultivate schism, or to separate in pride, Caleb stood his ground—in faith—but still moved in partnership and support. For the next forty years, he moved alongside many whose unbelief delayed his own experience of victory. See it, please. Here is tenacious patience as well as faith! His eventual actual possession of the land at a later date indicates that, even though delays come, faith's confession will ultimately bring victory to the believer.[3]

PETER

The healing of the lame man in Acts 3:1–16 offers another look at supernatural faith. Though many miracles occurred through the ministry of Peter, the methodology of this miracle is reported only here. It is significant for several reasons. Answer the following questions from the text:

1. How long had the lame man been in this condition?

2. Where was the lame man when Peter spoke to him?

3. What did Peter say he had to give the lame man?

4. How did he give this to him?

5. When was the man healed?

6. What, did Peter say, did **not** heal the man?

7. To what did Peter attribute this healing? (v. 16)

8. Where did this faith come from?

BEHIND THE SCENES

In this first recorded miracle performed by the disciples, we are given the key for use by all believers in exercising faith's authority. When commanding healing for the lame man, Peter employs the full name/title of our Lord: "Jesus Christ [Messiah] of Nazareth." "Jesus" ("Joshua" or "Yeshua") was a common name among the Jews and continues to be in many cultures today. But the declaration of His full name and title, a noteworthy practice in Acts, seems a good and practical lesson for us (see Acts 2:22; 4:10). Let us be complete when claiming our authority over sickness, disease, or demons. In our confession of faith or proclamation of power, confess His deity and His lordship as "the Christ" ("Messiah"); use His precious name, as "Jesus" ("Savior"). Call upon Him as "Lord Jesus" or "Jesus Christ" or "Jesus of Nazareth." There is no legal or ritual demand intended in this point, but it is wise to remember, even as we pray "in Jesus' name" (John 16:24), so we exercise all authority in Him—by the privilege of power He has given us in His name (Matt. 28:18; Mark 16:12; John 14:13, 14). Many other compound names for Him are found in the Word of God. Let us declare them in faith, with prayer and full confidence.[4]

Please note that the healing required a choice by Peter. He chose to extend his hand to the lame man and to pick him up. He chose to speak the healing words in the name of the Lord Jesus. But in responding to the amazement of everyone as they saw the lame man now walking, jumping, and praising God, Peter says that it was faith that healed him. And more important to our discussion, Peter declares that this faith "comes through Him (and) has given him this perfect soundness in the presence of you all."

Peter recognized that the operation of this faith was not premeditated. This faith is not a function of character or personal acquisition. Though *obedient* choice is certainly involved, Peter makes it clear that nothing of personal holiness, self-will, or personal power has accomplished this wonderful miracle (Acts 3:12).

Peter acknowledged that this miracle was made possible by a faith whose source is beyond human initiation. This supernatural faith can be and is to be cooperated with, it can be and is to be released through human agency, but above all, this faith "comes from Him!"

PAUL AND THE LAME MAN AT LYSTRA

Open your Bible to Acts 14:1–18, and examine it to answer these questions:

1. How did the Lord bear witness to the word of His grace?

2. How long had the lame man in Lystra been in that condition?

3. What did Paul command the man to do?

4. How did the lame man respond?

5. What did Paul see in the man?

Since Paul's habit, when entering a new city, was to speak to the Jewish community first, some have assumed that this lame man was a Jew. This cannot be known for certain, but it is most probable that he was hearing the "word of grace" for the first time. As Paul preaches about Jesus Christ, what His death and resurrection have accomplished for all, the lame man begins to believe.

It is vital to note that Paul was not preaching on healing. He was preaching *Christ*—that is, Jesus Himself as the prophesied Savior-King. When Paul sees faith in the lame man, he does not see faith to be healed. He sees faith in Christ—in Jesus the Lord. This man has begun to believe what Paul is saying about the Lord Jesus. When Paul recognizes the presence of faith, he gives the command, "Stand up straight on your feet!"

Remember from your study that the signs and wonders were promised and given by the Lord Jesus to bear witness to the message the apostles were preaching (Mark 16:15–20). This miracle occurs as a sign, bearing witness to the truth of Paul's presentation of Jesus Christ. Notice, too, that the sign occurs to one having faith.

Where did this faith come from?

The presence of faith in this man coincides with his hearing the *message* of Jesus Christ! It is the proclamation of the message of the Lord Jesus that awakens this faith, and it is the *working* of the Holy Spirit that makes faith available to this man who has never experienced strength in his feet before this moment.

 PROBING THE DEPTHS

This chapter on the "Gift of Faith" will be followed by the chapter, "The Choice of Faith." This is intentional. However, neither chapter is presented as an alternative. Some in the renewal movement within the church have become polarized on the question, "Is faith sovereign, or is faith all a matter of human choice?"

Two personalities from the early days of renewal illustrate the different positions: Charles Price and Smith Wigglesworth. Both were evangelists, Price from Canada and Wigglesworth from Great Britain.

Charles Price preached that all faith was a matter of the sovereignty of God. If you didn't have faith, there wasn't a thing you could do about it! Either you had it, or you didn't! Price said, "God will move, then you may follow." A story is told of the evangelist Price. A young man entered the church service late and was ushered to the front row. Though late, he noticed that the meeting hadn't yet started. He whispered to the man sitting next to him, "What, haven't we started? Where is the evangelist?" To his surprise, he heard, "Young man, I *am* the evangelist. But we are not starting until the Lord has arrived!"

Smith Wigglesworth believed quite differently. His message was, "*You* move, and then *God* will move!" He is famous for outlandish behavior. This story illustrates his position on matters of faith: He once pulled a woman from her wheelchair with the command, "Be healed!" Instead of being healed she fell down. Everyone else was quite embarrassed. Not Wigglesworth. He calmly put her back in the wheelchair and said, "Young woman, you fell because you tripped over your blankets." Again he pulled her from the wheelchair with the command to be healed. And she *was!*

Both men had extraordinary results in seeing many people healed, but their methodologies were quite different. Since both ministries occurred quite early in the renewal movement of this century, the church's understanding of faith and the miraculous was just beginning to be developed. Since then, many are tempted to, or actually do, polarize on the question of God's sovereignty vs. human participation. But when we're faced with the question today, "Is faith all God, or is faith all man?" the best answer is "both!" There is the *gift of faith* (from God, Who sovereignly gives), and there is the *choice of faith* (by man to actively receive).

Our faith life will be complete only if we will make room for both. Consider this: there will be times when God's Spirit will make it possible for you supernaturally to believe. The gift of faith will flow from within you, and in the face of difficult circumstances you will sense a solid confidence rising. Though nothing of your circumstance would agree with your sense of faith, you will hear or sense within yourself the saying, "This is going to be O.K. This will work out." Why do you feel this confidence? Because the Holy Spirit's presence is giving you the gift of faith.

But also consider those other moments: when the circumstances all are evaluated in the cold light of reality, and you feel no confidence. Yet, you may hear God's Word in your heart, whispering to your soul. Or perhaps a promise committed to memory long before will surface to your thinking. At this moment, you have a choice. You may give your faith to the practical diagnosis of the circumstance. Or, you may give your faith to the power-filled promises of God's Word. This is the type of setting when we all face the choice of faith.

 FAITH ALIVE

Write a personal experience you have had with the "gift of faith."

What are those things you can do that make you responsive to the working of the Holy Spirit who brings the manifestation of the gift of faith? (Eph. 5:18)

Romans 12:3–8, says that you have received a "measure" of faith. Everyone has. Honestly evaluate how you are using the measure of faith you have been given.

1. *Spirit-Filled Life Bible,* Jack Hayford, General Editor (Nashville, TN: Thomas Nelson Publishers, 1991), 1678.

1. Ibid., 213, "Word Wealth: Num. 13:30, able."

3. Ibid., 213, "Kingdom Dynamics: Num. 13:30; 14:6–9; "Faith When Facing Delays."

4. Ibid., 1629, "Kingdom Dynamics: Acts 3:6; Jesus' Name: Faith's Complete Authority."

Lesson 3/The Choice of Faith

It was raining hard. The interstate had narrowed to one lane because of construction. To make matters worse, I was following the only truck within a thousand miles. I wasn't happy.

They had called late at night from the camp our son was attending. "Pastor Hicks, we think your son has broken both his legs." My nine-year-old was two hours away. There wasn't a thing I could do about the distance or the accident that had happened. They needed permission to take him to the hospital. Of course I agreed, and asked how he was doing.

"He's in a great deal of pain and is crying," I was told. It didn't help my emotions. "Tell him his dad loves him, that I'm praying for him; that I'm on my way to meet you at the hospital," I said.

That had been an hour ago. And here I was, stuck behind what seemed to be the slowest trucker on the North American continent. I swerved behind him with my lights blinking to high intensity. Apparently, this signal was not well received by the inhabitant of the truck. He actually seemed to slow down and fully occupied the lane so as to make my passing an invitation to disaster.

A friend from the East Coast had been at the house and had volunteered to make the trip with me. He asked if he could pray. Better he than I! Because at this point, my emotions were all tilted towards the red indicators: I was *angry* at the trucker; *angry* at the camp; *angry* with the kids involved in the accident; *angry* with the counselor on whose watch the accident had happened; *angry* with myself for letting my kid attend the camp!

And, yes, I was even a little angry with the Lord for allowing this to happen to my son. After all, didn't He care? Didn't He know this was going to happen? Why didn't He keep it from happening? Yes, it was much better for my friend to pray.

As Amos prayed, the Holy Spirit began to convict me about the red indicators! As I processed the Holy Spirit's gracious conviction of my thoughts, I began to pray for each one I was angry with: the truck driver (I actually praised God for someone obeying the speed laws!), the camp director, the counselor, the other boys—myself. As I remember, it was somewhere North of Salem, Oregon, on I-5, that I asked the Lord to forgive me for the anger I had felt towards Him. It was foolish. I regretted it. And His forgiveness was instantaneous.

Then I joined Amos in praying for Jeff. Ill never forget the words that came out of my mouth: "Lord, I ask You to heal Jeff, but You don't have to. I would love a miracle, but I don't require one. You already have me lock, stock, and barrel. Lord, if I never see another miracle as long as I live, I've already seen enough of Your grace and power to convince me of who You are. Mighty God, be freed to do whatever You choose to do for your own purposes. For me, I choose to believe in You."

Later, Amos commented on the sense of the Lord's presence we both felt at that moment. For me, I knew another crucial faith test had just been passed. Every time you pass a faith test, you will discover the matter of choice. In fact, there is no way to pass a faith test without the issue of choice.

In this instance, I had passed the test of circumstances by *choosing* to believe **in** Him, as opposed to *believing* **for** Him to do something on my behalf.

Please understand, there is nothing wrong in believing for the miraculous. We are admonished to contend for the faith once given to the saints (Jude 1:3). However, we are never privileged to *require* the miraculous in order to decide if we'll continue to put our faith in the Lord Jesus.

Stuck behind that truck on a rainy night in Oregon, I had made a decisive faith choice. The Lord had blessed our small church in Eugene with many miracles and much growth. It was not unusual for us to see many people healed of all manner of sickness. In the church, there was an immense capacity for faith, an ability to believe for the miraculous. I was not a stranger to faith for the miraculous.

But now I asked myself, *Has something crept into my faith life? Has some Pharisaic contamination begun to express itself in my ministry?* I honestly do not know. But I do know this: the moment I said, "I do not require a miracle," something of God's glory broke across my inner being.

In that moment of glory, I began to pray for my son. I spoke peace into his heart, feeling confident God was doing it that moment, though I was miles away. I asked the Lord to comfort Jeff, and I also rebuked the enemy from using this incident to misshape him in any way.

When we arrived at the hospital, I was taken immediately to the emergency room. What did I discover? A smiling little boy, who jumped down from the cot and ran into my arms. I noticed two things: One, his legs were obviously not broken! And two, he was wearing the same clothes—unchanged from when he had left for camp five days before!

As we drove back home together, I asked him what happened. He responded, "Dad, I don't know. It hurt real bad, and then it just stopped hurting." To this day, I don't have the slightest idea what really happened. The nurse at the camp believed both legs were broken. A young man on the camp staff who had served in Vietnam as a medic had thought the same thing. There was no "absolute" medical confirmation, and so I say, "I don't know." But I do know this: I experienced the glory of the Lord when (1) I made a confession and was purified and forgiven of anger, (2) I made a faith choice that honored Him, and (3) I released God from my requirements of the miraculous. And further, I know that my son experienced something that he will never forget either. All this is enough.

CHOOSING TO BELIEVE

There are several incidents from the life of the Lord Jesus that illustrate the importance of choosing to believe. Read Mark 4:35–41. From this story of the storm, answer these questions:

1. What did Jesus say to his disciples to initiate the journey?

2. When the storm came, what was Jesus doing?

3. What does this suggest to you?

4. How did He deal with the storm?

5. The disciples heard Jesus speak to the storm. What did they hear Him say to them?

It is significant to note that Jesus rebuked both the storm and the disciples! Though He made the storm on the *outside* cease, He expected them to deal with the storm on the *inside*. As you read through the Gospel narratives, you will be surprised how often Jesus will control the elements and control demonic spirits—yet you will hardly ever see Him controlling the disciples. Only *He* could rebuke the storm on the sea of Galilee. Only *they* could rebuke the storm of fear and doubts they were experiencing.

When He asks, "Why is it that you have no faith?" He is suggesting that faith was possible—that it was a matter of choice. They could have chosen to believe instead of giving in to their doubts and fears.

This is true for us, too. In His wisdom, God has made you and me responsible in matters of faith. Only we can deal with doubts and fears. Use a concordance to see how many times the phrase "fear not" or "do not fear" is used in the Bible. The admonition would not be there if it were not possible. If Jesus says, "Fear not," it must be possible for us to receive that mastery over fear!

WORD WEALTH

Romans 8:15—". . . the spirit of bondage again to **fear.**" *Phobia, phobos, (Strong's #5401; fob-*oss); alarm or fright:— be afraid, exceedingly, fear, terror, from which comes *phebo-mai* (to be put in fear).

Paul associates this terror with the spirit of bondage, and writes that we have not been given that spirit. We have received the working of the Holy Spirit that is called the "spirit of adoption." He will lead us to exclaim, "Abba Father", an endearing term used by those who know that they are included in the family of God.

WORD WEALTH

Second Timothy 1:7—"God has not given us a spirit of **fear,**" *deilia (Strong's #1167;* di-*lee-*ah); timidity or fear.

As Paul confronts Timothy's fear, he reminds him what he has been given by the Holy Spirit. From 2 Timothy 1:7, what are the three things Paul says that Timothy has received from God?

1.

2.

3.

In the last lesson, we considered faith as a gift of the Holy Spirit. When we consider faith as a choice, let us never think that we are left alone! God's Spirit is working into us the knowledge that each of us is a child of the Father. By this means, the Holy Spirit is seeking to give us power, love, and a sound mind.

WORD WEALTH

Second Timothy 1:7—"**Sound mind**," *sophronismos* (*Strong's #4995;* so-fron-is-*mos*); discipline, i.e. self-control:—sound mind.

While the word *fear* means a timidity, loss of confidence, *sound mind* refers to the ability to be under control during difficult circumstance, to think straight under pressure. The bad news: there *is* a spirit of fear. That spirit was working on Timothy, and it will seek to work on you too. The good news: the Holy Spirit *is* making a *sound mind* available to you at the same time.

You can choose to believe. You can also choose to panic, giving in to doubts and fears. But the choice is yours. Using the metaphor of the story in Mark 4, if the Lord Jesus says, "Let us go over to the other side," it is reasonable to assume you will make it!

The question then becomes, "What has the Lord said to you?" Or perhaps better said, "What Scriptures do you know which may be applied to your current set of circumstances?"

If some aspects of faith are a matter of choice, and, if the choice is between what you know the Lord has said, and what your circumstances are saying—or what the enemy of your soul is saying—then knowing what the Lord is saying becomes extremely important!

WORD WEALTH

Romans 10:17—"So then faith comes by hearing, and hearing by the word of God." *Note:* "In God's ordinary means of operating, people do not come to saving faith unless they either read the Bible or have someone tell them the gospel message that is in it. It is the **Word of God** that the Spirit uses to awaken a response of faith within us, and it is the reliability of the Word of God on which we rest our faith for salvation.[1]

THE SPIRIT AND THE WORD

Where faith is a matter of choice, you can be confident that God's Spirit is speaking the Word upon which you may base your choice to believe. Again using the story of the storm from Mark 4, let us notice that the disciples had His word ("Let us go over to the other side"), and they also had His presence. (He was with them in the boat.) In comparison, then, answer these questions:

Is Jesus with you? Write your thoughts as you read these promises.

Matt. 28:20—"Teaching them to observe all things that I have commanded you; and lo, I am with you always, *even* to the end of the age." Amen.

Acts 18:10—"For I am with you, and no one will attack you to hurt you; for I have many people in this city."

He is with you! Armed by what He has spoken to you, make good choices—choices to believe. Be responsible in dealing with your doubts and fears. Remember, Jesus will rebuke the storm on the *out*side. Only you can rebuke the storm on the *in*side.

It is not responsible or necessarily even truthful to say, "I am not afraid." But it is responsible to say, "I will not be afraid." It is not responsible to say, "I do not have any doubts." It is responsible to say, "I will not give in to doubts."

Write these verses:

1. Psalm 56:3

2. Isaiah 12:2

3. Psalm 92:2 (Read vv. 1–6)

 PROBING THE DEPTHS

It is true that a certain form of faith has been taught in recent years that is more New Age than it is biblical. What are the differences?

- New Age faith teaching leads you down the pathway of getting your way. Biblical faith teaching leads you down the path of getting God's way!
- New Age faith teaching makes your will important. Biblical faith teaching makes God's will supremely important.
- New Age faith teaching employs tactics of denial, refusing to acknowledge the reality of personal, supernatural evil. Biblical faith teaching acknowledges reality and triumphs through the tragedy.

Denial is based in fear, but faith is never afraid of reality. Some people want to believe for healing because they are afraid of sickness. But biblical faith contends for healing because God has promised it ("I am the Lord who heals you."—Ex. 15:26), not because we fear the complications or implications of affliction or death.

This is not to suggest that a believer never fears, whether pain, sickness, poverty—or even the Enemy. Sincere, faithful believers experience fear of all these, but some adopt the art of denial, never admitting to fear, as though their denial is "faith." Genuine faith is centered in the Lord and His Word. It is based in Him—*the* Truth—and His Word which *is* truth (John 14:6; 17:7). Instead of living in a religious or philosophical world of denial, a biblical believer armed with faith's true understanding will refuse to be moved or to make decisions based on fear. That "true understanding" is (1) the Lord is with you, (2) His Word is true, and (3) He will not fail you or His Word.

Do you believe?

In the following four verses, Jesus asks the question, "Do you believe?" Write down your observations from each incident, being careful to study the context. In each case, see how Jesus calls for the *choice* of faith. That choice is not the power of faith. It is simply our accepting His promise—His Word. The power is His, the promise He's given to us. (Emphasis is added in each verse.)

1. Matthew 9:28—"And when He had come into the house, the blind men came to Him. And Jesus said to them, '*Do you believe* that I am able to do this?' They said to Him, 'Yes, Lord.'"

2. John 1:50—"Jesus answered and said to him, 'Because I said to you, "I saw you under the fig tree," *do you believe?* You will see greater things than these.'"

3. John 9:35—"Jesus heard that they had cast him out; and when He had found him, He said to him, '*Do you believe in the Son of God?*'"

4. John 11:26—"And whoever lives and believes in Me shall never die. *Do you believe* this?"

 FAITH ALIVE

In the previous lesson, you studied the *gift of faith.* God's Spirit can move powerfully in you so that faith is less a matter of *making* something happen and more a matter of *letting* something happen. Because it is a gift, you can only receive it. We each *can* respond to a gift being offered. We cannot initiate the offering of that gift, but we can receive it.

In this chapter, you have also studied the concepts behind faith as a *choice.* Evaluate your recent decisions in matters of faith in the following circumstances: Describe ways that

In my home, I am choosing to believe

In my job, I am choosing to believe

In my health, I am choosing to believe

In my emotions, I am choosing to believe

In my ministry, I am choosing to believe

This is a splendid exercise, but look back at what you have written. If you have written choices that express your desires, and not His will (as revealed in His Word), then you will experience something less of faith's power than He intends. Go over the areas again, and write in a Bible verse that you understand as addressing your circumstance. Make that promise the basis for your faith, and let God into your circumstance by that choice. *You* needn't feel it's *your* task to create or beget the power to bring solutions. Yours is simply to choose *Him*. *He* has the power, and He's given you and me His promise!

1. *Spirit-Filled Life Bible* (Nashville, TN: Thomas Nelson Publishers, 1991), note on Rom. 10:17.

Lesson 4/Faith and Healing

Crack! Third inning, two outs, and the kid at bat had just hit a pop fly over my head at shortstop. Eye on the ball, backpedaling furiously, I was going to make the final out of the inning. Unfortunately, the kid playing left field had the same idea. Everyone was amazed at the perfect timing of the event. I tripped. He fell on top of me. Neither of us caught the ball. Another typical day at your local Little League Baseball diamond.

Except for the fact that I had a broken collarbone, in two places, there went the summer! If I hadn't been in so much pain, I could have really been ticked off. But it hurt too much for that.

As they were taking me home, I realized I had another problem. Not only did I have a broken collarbone, I had a dad who believed in the Bible's promises of divine healing. By "divine healing" he meant, "The power of God to heal the sick and afflicted in answer to believing prayer offered in Jesus' name." My dad's faith for healing was so strong, our family experienced very little sickness. (In later years, my brother and I would say that we were "not permitted" to get sick!)

As the coach carried me into the living room, I was aware of my dad quietly asking questions. After the coach left, Dad spoke to me. He surprised me. I was expecting him to pray one of his famous "get-well" prayers, because that's what he usually did. (And it usually worked, too, not that I always wanted it to. Other kids could occasionally stay home with a tummy ache. Not us! "Be healed in Jesus' name! Now, go to school.")

But this time, I heard him say, "Well, Son, what would you like to do?" *Unfair,* I thought. *Just pray, and make this better. Quick.*

From the look in his eye, I knew he had made a decision—that this was going to be *my* choice. Only years later would I realize that he understood how strategic it was for a growing son to come to a time of grappling on his own with God's promises and covenants of healing.

So, made bold by all the other times he had prayed, I said, "Just pray, Dad." He did. And when I tried to move my arm, it hurt! Instead of praying again, he just smiled. I remember him telling me that he would take me to the doctor as soon as I was ready to go.

Now there was an interesting proposition. I'd never met a doctor, or been in a hospital, let alone have one actually work on me. It was not a pleasant thought. So, based more on fear of the unknown than faith in the Lord, I chose to employ a homemade arm sling and went upstairs to bed. I was eleven and much more caught up in the pleasures of summer that I envisioned slipping away than I was in giving the Lord glory through the healing process.

But something happened in those two weeks that has influenced me for the rest of my life. I actually read the Bible—seriously and personally for my growth. Like most good little church kids, I had memorized Scripture for contests, and in general, to show off in front of the adults. But I had not actually read the Bible's promises for any other purpose. It was not connected to "real life!"

Now it was. Especially after I fell down the stairs the next day, and the entire neighborhood heard me yell out my pain. Suddenly the doctor sounded like a good idea. Dad still said the same thing, "What would you like to do?"

As an eleven-year-old, I made a decision based on an admittedly immature understanding of God's purpose and promises, but nonetheless I chose to believe for healing. How I know He healed me is the "rest of the story." Before I tell you that, let's review some of the healing promises that will build your faith.

HEALING PROVISION

The prophet Isaiah describes the Lord Jesus as the Suffering Servant. In chapter 53, Isaiah portrays graphically the suffering of our Lord upon the cross. Study Isaiah 53:1–12, using these questions as you read through the verses:

1. How is the Lord's appearance described in verse 2?

2. What does He carry, and with what is He acquainted in verse 3?

3. According to verse 4, how was the Lord esteemed?

4. According to verse 4, what did the Lord bear?

5. According to verse 5, why was the Lord wounded?

6. According to verse 5, why was the Lord bruised?

7. According to verse 5, what did His stripes accomplish?

8. According to verse 6, what has the Lord done with our iniquity?

9. According to verse 7, what response does the Lamb give in His suffering?

10. According to verse 8, why was He stricken?

11. According to verse 10, what phrase appears to refer to the Lord's resurrection?

12. According to verse 11, how shall the Righteous Servant justify many?

13. According to verse 12, what four things did the Servant do for mankind?

   WORD WEALTH

Isaiah 53:4, **Griefs,** *choliy* (*Strong's* #2483; khol-*ee*); from malady, anxiety, calamity:—disease, grief, sickness. Use a Bible concordance to look up this word to see how many times it is used to refer to physical sickness.

   WORD WEALTH

Isaiah 53:4, **Sorrows,** *makob* (*Strong's* #4341; mak-*obe*). This word is often translated "sorrow," "grief," and seems to refer to emotional pain, while the preceding word seems to refer to physical pain. Use a concordance to see how the word is employed by other writers.

KINGDOM EXTRA

Dr. N. M. Van Cleave writes on this text: "Isaiah 53 clearly teaches that bodily healing is included in the atoning work of Christ, His suffering, and His Cross. The Hebrew words for 'griefs' and 'sorrows' (v. 4) specifically means physical affliction. This is verified in the fact that Matthew 8:17 says this Isaiah text is being exemplarily fulfilled in Jesus' healing people of human sickness and other physical need.

"Further, that the words 'borne' and 'carried' refer to Jesus' atoning work on the Cross is made clear by the fact that they are the same words used to describe Christ's bearing our sins (see v. 11; also 1 Pet. 2:24). These texts unequivocally link the grounds of provision for both our salvation and our healing to the atoning work of Calvary. Neither is automatically appropriated however; for each provision—a soul's salvation or a person's temporal, physical healing—must be received by faith. Christ's work on the Cross makes each possible: simple faith receives each as we choose.

"Incidentally, a few contend that Isaiah's prophecy about sickness was fulfilled completely by the one-day healings described in Matthew 8:17. A close look, however, will show that the word 'fulfill' often applies to an action that extends throughout the whole church age." (See Is. 42:1–4; Matt. 12:14–17; Ps. 107:20; Matt. 4:23–25).[1]

 AT A GLANCE

Before you study some other important scriptures outlining God's provision for your physical well-being, take the time to look at this chart which combines verses from Isaiah 52 and 53, and lists references from the New Testament which fulfill them.

THE SUFFERING SERVANT

Jesus understood His mission and work as the fulfillment of Isaiah's Suffering Servant.

The Prophecy	The Fulfillment
He will be exalted (52:13).	Philippians 2:9
He will be disfigured by suffering (52:14; 53:2).	Mark 15:17, 19

The Prophecy	The Fulfillment
He will make a blood atonement (52:15).	1 Peter 1:2
He will be widely rejected (53:1, 3).	John 12:37,38
He will bear our sins and sorrows (53:4, 5).	Romans 4:25; 1 Peter 2:24, 25
He will be our substitute (53:6, 8).	2 Corinthians 5:21
He will voluntarily accept our guilt and punishment (53:7, 8).	John 10:11; 19:30
He will be buried in a rich man's tomb (53:9).	John 19:38–42
He will save us who believe in Him (53:10, 11).	John 3:16; Acts 16:31
He will die on behalf of transgressors (53:12).	Mark 15:27, 28; Luke 22:37[2]

God's loving, healing provision is rooted in the atoning work of the Son of God upon the Cross, the power of God through the Holy Spirit's ministry, and the character of God, which is committed to seeking human wholeness. Put another way, by nature God is a healing God. In terms of power, there is nothing impossible with Him. And legally, the work of Christ on the Cross opens the door for a Holy God to administer His healing mercies to a people who would otherwise be unqualified to receive His healing touch.

HEALING PROMISES

In the following verses, what does the Lord say He will heal?

1. 2 Chronicles 7:14

2. Psalms 6:2, 3

3. Psalm 41:4

4. Isaiah 57:17, 18; Jeremiah 3:22; Hosea 14:4

5. Isaiah 61:1

6. Jeremiah 30:17

Every promise has a condition. Study the following verses in their context. Write out the healing promise, and the condition which must be met for that promise of healing to be kept.

1. Isaiah 58:8
   Promise:

   Condition:

2. Exodus 23:25
   Promise:

   Condition:

3. Deuteronomy 7:15
   Promise:

   Condition:

4. James 5:14, 15
   Promise:

   Condition:

HEALING AND THE MINISTRY OF JESUS

There is no greater stimulus for us to gain faith for healing than the ministry of Jesus. Hebrews 13:8 says, "Jesus Christ is the same yesterday, today, and forever." This Wonderful One who is the same today as when He ministered the marvelous and powerful healings recorded in each of the four Gospels, invites you and me to trust Him for His healing touch!

Write your thoughts on the following four incidents of healing miracles performed by the Lord Jesus. What impresses you about *Him?* What speaks to you about yourself?

1. Matthew 12:10–13

2. Mark 2:1–12

3. Luke 4:38–43

4. John 4:47–54

HEALING CONTINUED THROUGH THE CHURCH

PROBING THE DEPTHS

It is taught by some that faith for healing is improper. They base their view in large part on the proposition that once the Scriptures were *canonized,* i.e., once the Bible as we know it was fully assembled, there was and is no longer a need for the miraculous; that now, evidence for faith by an individual should "rest solely upon the Scriptures." This view holds that the healing ministry of the Lord Jesus through the church ceased with the passing away of the last apostles.

In answering this objection, let's first assert that the view being presented through *this* study guide totally agrees that our faith must rest entirely upon the Scriptures, for the Bible says, "Faith cometh by hearing, and hearing by the Word of God" (Rom. 10:17, KJV).

At the same time, however, the Scriptures themselves do not teach a cessation of the healing provision God has made available to mankind. The idea of the "cessation" of healing, miracles (or any of the Spirit's gifts) appears to be a manmade proposition, based on human opinion and church dogma, plus the interpretation some give to their negative personal experiences.

 ## BEHIND THE SCENES

One claim for a biblical "proof text" opposing the present-day miraculous works of God is in First Corinthians 13:10. Supposing to glorify the importance of the Scriptures, human ingenuity has proposed that "that which is perfect" is the Bible—and since it has been completed, thereby all miracles and signs the New Testament holds forth are "passed away" or occurring no longer. The Word of God reveals something quite different: "that which is perfect" refers to the completion of God's purposes through and beyond the coming of the Lord Jesus Christ (Rom. 8:18, 19). That is when all of God's fullest will for us will be realized. "There is no reason other than human opinion to presume to attribute this reference to the conclusion of the canon of the Scriptures. While the inspired Word of God was completed at the end of the first century, its completion did not signal an end to the continuing operation of the very powers it describes. Nor did it signal the end of human need for compassion and healing. Rather, that Word instructs us to welcome the Holy Spirit's gifts and ministries in our lives, to round out our sufficiency for ministry to a needy world—through the Word *preached* and the Word *confirmed.*"[3]

Write your thoughts and observations from the following texts which describe the Lord's healing ministry through the church. Note different things that happen and *how* the healing grace of God is ministered.

1. Acts 3:1–11; Acts 4:14

2. Acts 5:15, 16

3. Acts 8:7

4. Acts 9:36–42

5. Acts 19:12–17

6. Acts 28:8, 9

7. Philippians 2:26, 27

Review the above and remember: Jesus was alive and ministered healing through the first century church. Jesus is *alive* to minister healing *today*—to you and through you!

You have studied Old Testament prophecies presenting the atoning work of Jesus Christ on the Cross. In that section, you studied the scriptural references that included God's provision for your physical well being as well as your spiritual well-being. We reenforced the truth that the work of Christ on the Cross is the legal basis upon which God extends His healing mercies to believers who have become justified through their faith in Christ.

You have also studied promises for healing, all of which have conditions. These conditions are matters of faith and obedience. When fully met, these conditions position believers *not* to issue a *demand* upon God, but to come under the *hand* of God in a place where they are able to receive the working out of His promise in their experience.

In studying the accounts of the Lord Jesus' healing ministry, you have encountered the unchanging One, Who is the same yesterday, today, and forever. You can have faith **in** Him to be your healing Lord today. He does not change.

In studying the healing incidents that continued through the church after the ascension of the Lord Jesus, you have seen that the provision of healing continues and is to be continued not only **to** you, but **through** you to a needy world.

THE REST OF THE STORY

In concluding this lesson on faith and healing, I'd like to finish the story I began in the introduction.

Two weeks later, in a childhood fight with a neighborhood friend, I was knocked out and taken to the hospital by the lucky puncher's mother. The doctor quickly confirmed my claim that it was a "lucky" punch. But before he could release me, I heard the mother say, "Doctor, as long as we're here, would you check that boy's collarbone? I think it's been broken, and I'm not sure it was cared for properly."

Quickly, the doctor probed my collarbone. I'll never forget what he said. "Son, your collarbone has been broken in two places and has set perfectly." Probably provoked by the lady's question, he then asked, "What did you do for it?" I smiled weakly and said, "We just prayed."

He laughed and said, "Whatever you did, you're fine. Just try to avoid those sucker punches from now on!"

On the way home, my friend's mother apologized. She told me that the rest of the neighborhood had been quite upset with our family, thinking that I was not being cared for properly. This would not be the last time I would hear a doctor confirm the wonderful working of God's healing mercies in our family.

Looking back, though I am grateful for the doctor's words, I am more grateful for a father who was wise enough to let me have my first faith experience for healing in a loving environment. He didn't *force* me to faith, but let me choose to trust. He made a trip to the doctor immediately available, without the thought of its being an unworthy or unacceptable choice. In short, he made *me* decide what *I* believed rather than let my faith be dependent upon his.

I've always been grateful for those moments when I looked to the Scriptures for the first time to base my personal faith on something God was saying personally to me!

 FAITH ALIVE

Take the time to write out the promises for healing that have come alive to you during your study through this lesson. What conditions must be met in order for your faith to move "under God's hand"—to become fully released to receive these promises?

1. *Spirit-Filled Life Bible* (Nashville, TN: Thomas Nelson Publishers, 1991), "Kingdom Dynamics: Is. 53:4, 5, Healing Prophesied Through Christ's Atonement," 1032.

2. Ibid., 1033, Chart: "The Suffering Servant, Is. 53:12."

3. Ibid., 1739, note on 1 Cor. 13:10.

Lesson 5/Faith and the Miraculous

Jesus said, "And these signs shall follow them that believe; In my name shall they cast out devils; they shall speak with new tongues; They shall take up serpents; and if they drink any deadly thing, it shall not hurt them; they shall lay hands on the sick, and they shall recover (Mark 16:17, 18; KJV).

John records that the promise to continue the ministry of the miraculous through the disciples was spoken to them on the night Jesus was betrayed. "Verily, verily, I say unto you, He that believeth on me, the works that I do shall he do also; and greater *works* than these shall he do; because I go unto my Father" (John 14:12; KJV).

In both cases, the continuation of the miraculous is based on the condition of believing. In some parts of the church, it is taught that miracles ceased sometime during the first century. It is thought that, with the death of the last of the original apostles and the completion of the canon, miracles are no longer necessary. However, this is never actually taught anywhere in the Scriptures. The Scriptures teach that the presence or absence of *faith* sets the tone for the relative possibilities of the miraculous.

In this chapter, we will review eleven miracles in the ministry of the Lord Jesus. In each miracle, you will find a specific mention of either faith, an act of believing, or an admonition to believe. Before commencing the study, here are three observations which might be helpful to you.

Observation One: *The miraculous has been an integral part of every era of God's revelation to His people.* Wherever the Scriptures serve as guardians of history, i.e., the ancient kingdoms of Judah and Israel, the reigns of the prophets and judges, the period of the Exile, and the return of Israel to rebuild the Jerusalem walls and the temple—all are interwoven with some expressions of the miraculous.

The era of the patriarchs, the account of Moses' leadership, and the story of Joshua's possessing the Promised Land are filled with records of physical miracles, spiritual visitations, signs, wonders, and miracles of every kind. There were seasons when the Word of the Lord was rare; "there was no open vision" (1 Sam. 1:1). This rarity (in some translations, the word "rare" is translated "precious" to denote "unusual") is brought about by the unbelieving or disobedient character of God's people; not by the character of God—as though He became stingy with His loving displays of power.

Indeed, the One "with whom there is no variation or shadow of turning" (James 1:17) seems to be aggressive in displaying His power on behalf of those who will believe. Write out 2 Chronicles 16:9, and be reminded of this.

Observation Two: *Miracles are manifestations of God's glory, and are for His glory.* When Jesus changes the water into wine at the wedding at Cana, John says, "This beginning of signs Jesus did in Cana of Galilee, and manifested His **glory**" (John 2:11).

Every miracle is a manifestation of the glory of God. John uses this expression to describe this water-to-wine miracle, for some might not see it in the same category as a resurrection, the healing of a blind man, or the casting out of a demon. It is so kind—the assisting of a wedding reception's success—some could think it a "waste" of God's power; perhaps that's why John makes the statement he does. But regardless of the type of miracle, no matter what kind of "sign," it flows to manifest the glory of the Lord; that is, the excellence of His love, grace, mightiness, and power.

Every miracle is also *for* His glory, that *all* praise, *all* honor is to be given to Him, and *only* to Him when the miraculous occurs. As you study this lesson, you will see how many times the Lord Jesus commends individuals for their faith. It is good for us to see Him do this, for it indicates His delight—God's pleasure—with people "believing" in a way that welcomes and allows Him to do what unbelief would otherwise hinder.

As faith develops, it accesses the grace of God for the miraculous. Yet whenever the miraculous is released, even though humankind—you, someone you are praying for, or anyone else— benefited, it is *always* for God's glory.

Read Isaiah 42:8. What will the Lord not share?

Specifically, what will He not allow His praise to be given to?

Human nature inevitably worships the *human* agent through whom God's miracles might flow. It is also our nature not only to praise the one God uses to work a miracle, but the miracle itself, or artifacts associated with the miracle. The ancient church has venerated objects associated with past miracles, supposing that there is some efficacy in the object. This human tendency has a history, even in the Bible.

Turn to Numbers 21:4–9 and compare the story of how God healed the Israelites from the plague of fiery serpents with 2 Kings 18:1–4. See how that instrument of deliverance had become an object of worship. See how in order for true worship to be restored to the temple, this object had to be destroyed!

Aimee Semple McPherson, an evangelist of the 1930s, powerfully used by God in the ministry of the miraculous, had a biblical slogan engraved on her pulpit in Los Angeles. It read, "We would see Jesus" (John 12:21). She understood this imperative as one who regularly participated in the miraculous. This scripture, and the lessons above, are means to help us remember: the miraculous is a manifestation of God's glory and is always intended for His glory!

Observation Three: *The miraculous is always tied to God's eternal purpose.* While miracles which alleviate human need and suffering may, and often do, occur, ultimately the miracle is not merely about the human condition, but is linked to God's divine agenda.

Read Mark 16:17–18 again. Now, see the direct association with verse 15. The text gives the promise of the miraculous, but it also reveals its purpose: It is for the advance of the
gospel of salvation. Signs and wonders are given to confirm
the preaching of God's Word (v. 20).

Miracles are not available to help you or me get what we
want: They are for the purpose of enabling God to accomplish
what He wants to do! This gentle correction doesn't mean
God cares only for His *program* and not for *people*. Nothing
could be further from the truth, because people *are* God's
program. But we need to keep the focus on Him. He's the
fountain of love and power, and also the only One with all wisdom and understanding. We need to trust *Him* and call on
Him with *His* purpose being our highest concern.

Read 1 Peter 5:7. Upon what basis are you invited to
place your cares before God?

For an example of this balance of God's *purpose* and His
miracle *power*, read Exodus 3:9. This is where God called
Moses at the burning bush. In this encounter, Moses hears
God say, "The cry of the Israelites has come up to me; and I
have seen the oppression of the Egyptians." On the one hand
God's compassion is desirous of *delivering* Israel; on the other,
He is ready to move in judgment against Egyptian arrogance.

The student of biblical history realizes that God has committed Himself to the Israelites as His chosen people, and that
delivering them from Egypt was an integral part of His eternal
plan. At the same time God is fulfilling His eternal purpose in
revealing His global redemption plan, He is compassionately
ministering to the needs of His people.

Seeing this, let us be convinced we are not forced to
decide whether God is more interested in His eternal purpose
than in the human condition. He is concerned with both. Miracles display the grace of God to meet human need, and they
reveal the glory of God by fulfilling His purpose.

Why is this point so pivotal for us to understand? Because
the moment that we remove the subject of the miraculous

from a perception of God's eternal purpose, either Satan or human nature will attempt to harness the results of the miraculous for purposes of gain and deception!

Having made this third observation, let us review. Write your personal comments under each point:

1. Miracles have never ceased where there is faith.

2. Miracles are manifestations of God's glory and are manifested for His glory.

3. Miracles are always tied to God's eternal purpose.

JESUS' WORKING MIRACLES

Now, let's begin our examination of the eleven miracles we mentioned earlier.

As you study the following verses that describe certain miracles of the Lord Jesus, write out your own observations as to the importance of faith, noting the manner in which words or actions of faith are expressed and the ways in which faith is called forth or prompted.

Mark 2:1–12: The healing of the paralytic who was lowered through the roof.

1. What did Jesus see? (verse 5)

2. Why did Jesus forgive the paralyzed man before healing him?

Luke 7:1–10: The healing of the centurion's servant.

1. Upon what did the centurion base his faith?

2. What comment did the Lord make about the centurion's faith?

Mark 5:24–34: The healing of the woman with the issue of blood. (Examine the other Gospel accounts of this miracle: Matt. 9:20–22; Luke 8:43–48)

What did Jesus say made the woman well?

PROBING THE DEPTHS

It is obvious from this story that the miracle has not occurred with the conscious participation of the Lord Jesus. Since He asked, "Who touched Me?" we may assume that He honestly did not know. This is not to suggest that a miracle was taken from the Lord without His blessing. However, the story does seem to indicate that there is some dimension of the Lord's virtue that is available to the believer who will *press through* the throng (i.e., the circumstances), and *touch the Lord* for a miracle.

How did the Lord know that someone had touched him while He was in the midst of a multitude?

Matthew 9:27–31: The healing of the two blind men.

What question did the Lord ask before healing them of their blindness?

Matthew 14:23–33: The miracle of Peter walking on water.

1. What was the disciples' initial cry when they saw Jesus coming on the water?

2. What was Peter's response?

3. What caused Peter to become afraid?

4. How did the Lord chastise Peter?

Matthew 15:22–28: The deliverance of the Canaanite woman's daughter.

1. On what basis did the Lord surrender to the woman's request?

2. What does this instance suggest regarding faith's privilege to pursue God's promises in hope?

Mark 5:35–43: The Raising of Jairus's daughter.

1. How did the Lord admonish the ruler of the synagogue when news of his daughter's death was brought to them?

2. Who did the Lord cast out of the ruler's house?

3. Why do you think He did this, and what application might there be?

Luke 18:35–43: The healing of the blind man at Jericho.

1. What was the crowd's response to the blind man? And, what was the blind man's response to their words?

2. What did Jesus say saved the man?

 WORD WEALTH

Saved, *sodzo* (*Strong's #4982; sode*-zo). To save, deliver, or protect. Translated: to heal, to preserve, to save, to do well, to be made whole. For most believers, the concept of salvation is limited to the forgiveness of sins. As wonderful as forgiveness is, salvation is much, much more. To be saved, in the biblical sense of the word, is to be brought into wholeness. To be made whole is to experience life as God designed it to be lived. Salvation, or wholeness, is available only through faith.

Mark 9:17–29: The deliverance of the son from the dumb spirit.

1. Why could the disciples not cast out this spirit?

2. What did Jesus say to the spirit?

3. What did Jesus promise to the man if he would believe?

4. What was the man's response?

 KINGDOM EXTRA

Mark 9:22, 23. In this passage Jesus tells us that "believing" is the condition for answered prayer for a healing. The father of the demon-possessed boy answered in tears, "I believe," then added, "help my unbelief!" Since faith is a gift, we may pray for it as this father did. Note how quickly God's grace answered; but there is another lesson. Where an atmosphere of unbelief makes it difficult to believe, we should seek a different setting. Even Jesus' ability to work miracles was reduced where unbelief prevailed (Matt. 13:58).

Prayer and praise provide an atmosphere of faith in God. In this text Jesus explained yet another obstacle to faith's victory—why their prayers had been fruitless: This kind can come out by nothing but prayer and fasting (Mark 9:29). His explanation teaches: (1) some (not all) affliction is demonically imposed; and (2) some kinds of demonic bondage do not respond to exorcism, but only to fervent prayer. Continuance in prayer, accompanied by praise and sometimes fasting, provides a climate for faith that brings deliverance.[1]

John 4:46–54: The healing of the nobleman's son.

1. When did the nobleman believe that his son would be healed?

2. Having believed for his son's healing, what second act of faith did the nobleman commit?

 WORD WEALTH

Write out Psalm 107:20 as a cross-reference to the healing of the nobleman's son.

God's "sending His Word" occurs in two respects: *First,* God has sent His Word in that He has sent His Son. Jesus is the Word (John 1:14), and of His fullness have we all received (John 1:16). *Second,* God has sent His Word in the sense that He has given us the Scriptures—the written Word of God. As we believe His promises, we become open to the possibilities of His grace fulfilling those promises. What three things does Isaiah 55:11 say will happen when God "sends His Word"?

John 11:1–45: The raising of Lazarus from the dead.

1. List the five times Jesus uses the word "believe."

2. What did Jesus say is necessary in order to see the glory of God? (v. 40)

3. Why did Jesus pray at the grave of Lazarus as He did?

We have considered eleven miracles the Lord performed, all of which were released by the faith of the people involved. To conclude our study, read Mark 6:5, 6.

Why could the Lord not do mighty works at this time?

Miracles are released and received by faith. They are useful for the presentation of the gospel. A miracle may solve a human dilemma or mend a human condition. Whenever a miracle occurs, all praise and honor should be given to the Lord who performed it.

 FAITH ALIVE

Write out a miracle of God you have witnessed or experienced in a past season of your life—recent or distant. How did your faith align with or open to the miracle? How did you give the Lord glory and honor for this miracle? In the light of your study, is there a prayer you would like to make to God concerning His miraculous grace and power and your own life and service to Him? Write it out.

1. *Spirit-Filled Life Bible* (Nashville, TN: Thomas Nelson Publishers, 1991), "Kingdom Dynamics: Mark 9:22, 23, Cultivating a Climate of Faith for Healing," 1486.

Lesson 6/Faith and Suffering

It was a Sunday morning ministry time. Some of the elders and pastoral staff had joined me at the altar to minister to people desiring prayer. I hadn't intentionally eavesdropped, but one of the elders just happened to say it at a moment when I could hear. "My dear, none of us suffer very well. Use this moment of suffering to bring honor to your Lord."

When we were finished, I asked my friend what he had said and why. It wasn't offensive to me. But then, when people came forward for prayer, our custom would be to relieve suffering, not extend it! We administered gifts of healing, not gifts of suffering. Since I trusted him, at the time I was more amused and curious than anything else. But that changed.

I've never forgotten the incident. The Lord made sure I wouldn't, because for weeks to follow, His Holy Spirit drew me to the Scriptures. Repeatedly, it seemed I was being virtually forced to see the biblical models for suffering, and at the same time to review my own propensity for doing everything possible to avoid pain—any kind of pain or difficulty.

During that season that I saw how much of my faith was motivated by fear. In more instances than I cared to admit, I pursued powerful faith because I was afraid: afraid to be sick, afraid to be poor, afraid to be sad, afraid of disease. Afraid. Fear can be a powerful motivator. But as I was having to face this in myself, I was forced to own up to the fact that the Lord hasn't given us that spirit. Second Timothy 1:7 teaches, "For God has not given us a spirit of fear, but of power and of love and of a sound mind."

Let me invite you to a study in which we will review the Bible's teachings on suffering. First, think with me on the three major arenas of life in which the Bible reveals that believers will suffer: (1) Our suffering of persecution; (2) Our suffering of dealing with fallen nature; and (3) Our suffering of living on a planet dominated by the curse of sin.

In each of these dimensions of suffering, there is a special provision of grace that God offers—grace that can empower the believer to be *victorious* over and beyond the suffering rather than to be *victimized* by it.

To begin, our discerning the difference between being *victorious* and being a *victim* is important. God will help us when we are the victim, for His love reaches out to all those who have been in any way victimized by any aspect of suffering. Still, there is no biblical reason to believe that in any circumstance God intends for us as His children to be anything less than victorious overcomers.

Romans 8:35–39 is perhaps the best place to begin your study. Read these verses and answer these questions.

A. List the seventeen things which the Apostle Paul, inspired by the Holy Spirit, said *cannot* separate us from the love of God which is in Christ the Lord.

1	2	3
4	5	6
7	8	9
10	11	12
13	14	15
16	17	

B. The phrase, "through Him who loved us," makes it possible for the believer to be what kind of person?

C. From the preceding verses, 31 and 32, what statements can begin and sustain the believer's confession of faith in the face of all suffering, trial, or difficulty?

D. Write out your thoughts on Romans 8:32.

Grounded in the knowledge that *nothing* can separate you from the love of God in Christ Jesus, let's look at some of the words used in the verses on suffering.

WORD WEALTH

Suffering, *pathema* (*Strong's #3804; path*-ay-mah); something undergone, i.e., hardship or pain; subjectively, an emotion or influence: translated as affection, affliction, motion, suffering.

Pathos (*Strong's #3806; path*-os); properly, suffering ("pathos"), i.e., (subjectively) a passion; translated as (inordinate) affection, lust.

Pascho (*Strong's #3958; pas*-kho); to experience a sensation or impression (usually painful): translated as feel, passion, suffer, vex.

Sumpascho (*Strong's #4841; soom-pas*-kho); to experience pain jointly or of the same kind (specifically, persecution; to "sympathize"): translated as suffer with.

SUFFERING AND PERSECUTION

Read 2 Timothy 3:12. When Paul wrote to Timothy, whom he had left at Ephesus to pastor the growing church, he summoned the young man to be strong in the face of persecution. Now, read the context: verses 3:10–11. We are reminded of the price that Paul had paid to preach the gospel. As he wrote Timothy, all of us are thereby and to this day taught that when the believers set their lives on a course of holy living, there will be resistance!

 WORD WEALTH

Persecute, *dioko* (*Strong's #1377;* dee-*o*-ko); to pursue (literally or figuratively); by implication, to persecute; translated as ensue, follow (after), given to, suffer persecution, press forward. The word picture is of a relentless enemy's pursuit: someone is chasing you and will not give up.

Second Timothy 3:12 is often used to warn believers of the persecution they will suffer when following Christ. However, in the preceding verse, (2 Tim. 3:11), Paul also says two things that are critical to our understanding and action when we face such suffering.

- *I endured them!* This is not the tone of a victim. Paul is not lamenting. He is being honest with the facts of persecution. He has not surrendered to the feelings of persecution! He drew on God's grace and "went through."
- *The Lord delivered me from every one of them!* Hear it! Paul's experience is a model for you and me. For every believer who encounters persecution the message is clear— if you suffer persecution for your faith and godly living, Jesus Himself will deliver you!

Look up these verses, paying attention to their context, and write out your thoughts on what it means to suffer persecution for the gospel.

1. 2 Timothy 1:12

2. Galatians 5:11

3. Galatians 6:12

4. John 15:20

5. 1 Thessalonians 2:14, 15

6. Matthew 13:21

7. 1 Peter 4:15, 16

SUFFERING AND OUR FALLEN NATURE

Have you read any of the stories of the Anchorites? They were the hermits for Christ who lived in the third and fourth centuries and were remarkable men and women who committed themselves to a life-style of poverty and personal disadvantage in order to become holy. They thought that the way to holiness could be found only through the extreme circumstance of isolation and physical suffering.

Though I admire their tenacity, and many of their stories are quite remarkable, the Scriptures nowhere teach or require us to pursue or accept this kind of suffering. Rather, the Scriptures do teach that no one can commit themselves to winning personal victories over sin without suffering. A victory requires a battle: even a victorious battle involves suffering. How can we learn to meet this call to balance—to know there *will* be suffering to endure, but moving through it in confidence of victory ahead?

Read 1 Peter 2:11–17. Notice how, as Peter writes to us as "pilgrims" of faith, he encourages us to arm ourselves in our minds for the fight against sin. Though this passage also is connected to persecution, Peter's admonition deals most directly with that suffering which we face essentially because we have chosen to live differently than we did before we came to Christ.

This addresses the suffering we will face in dealing with our fallen human nature. It comes in two forms: interior and exterior. Times of temptation come to you and me just as surely as the Enemy came to our Lord Jesus Christ (Luke 4:1–13). But even when we don't experience any external stimulus towards sin, we all still have a fallen nature that can taunt us—a "self-life" that is completely capable of assailing us, and at times even sounding just like the tempter!

There is a promise in James 1:12–15, where we are presented a case study about the **Rewards** we will receive when we overcome temptation. What are they? At the same time, what **Reason** are we given why we as believers face this kind of suffering (vv. 13–14)?

 WORD WEALTH

Temptation, *peirazo* (*Strong's #3985;* pi-*rad*-zo); to test (objectively), i.e., endeavor, scrutinize, entice, discipline: translated as assay, examine, go about, prove, tempt, try.

Read 1 Corinthians 10:13. This power-filled promise enables every believer to have confidence in dealing with temptation. First, no temptation will ever come your way unless you will be able—if you *choose*—to deal with it properly. As a loving parent who would not let his child ride a bike until she has first learned to walk, your Lord will not allow you to face temptations which are beyond your abilities.

Second, your Lord will *always* provide a way of escape (Greek *ekbasis;* an exit, a way out). Whenever He permits you to be tested, He'll provide a way out! And third, God's design in making the exit available is not to promote our weakness, but to build our strength! The words ". . . that you may be able to bear it . . ." includes our word power, from the Greek word *dunamis*. You will be *empowered* to bear the test.

Let's review the promise: (1) We'll never be tested beyond our ability to resist. (2) We'll never be tested without an escape route being provided. (3) We'll never be tested except that He will fully empower us to stand firm and strong.

That's a powerful promise. However, while it does offer an escape, it also implies that there is no escaping the suffering that comes from dealing with temptation! How should the believer prepare for this kind of suffering? Read 1 Peter 4:1–5, and answer these questions:

1. Who has ceased from sin?

2. What are we to arm ourselves with, and what does this mean to you?

3. How are we to live the rest of our time?

In the light of your study of suffering and temptation, take time to read the following texts thoughtfully and to write your own observations on these verses that have to do with personal growth and victory over sin:

1. Hebrews 5:8

2. Hebrews 11:24, 25

3. Hebrews 12:1–4

4. Romans 8:16–18

5. Romans 8:26–28

6. Romans 12:21

7. Galatians 4:19—Notice that some suffering is on behalf of others, that they might win the battle over sin and self. Write some ways you have experienced this if you ever have.

8. 1 Corinthians 9:24–27 (See how even another form of suffering can be a self-imposed discipline in order to be victorious—"No pain—No gain!") Have you observed this in another mature Christian, or have you experienced it?

SUFFERING AND LIFE ON A FALLEN PLANET

A study of these verses can help us catch the attitude of the early church in dealing with the realities of a world stained with the curse of sin. Write out your thoughts, especially making a note of the "promise" that distills in your thoughts as you read these verses.

1. Romans 8:19–22

2. 1 Corinthians 4:11–13

 PROBING THE DEPTHS

Some teach that a true believer should never experience sickness. But even though you are a true believer, regardless of how strong your faith may be, you are likely to encounter sickness.

Read Philippians 2:26–30. The story of Epaphroditus is precious. His sickness apparently came as a result of the ministry assignment he had received. People who are devoted to serving others and to Christ-exalting ministry still get sick. Though they are strong in personal faith and associated with those who regularly experience the miraculous (that would certainly be true of Paul!), God does not promise a life free of the trial of sickness.

That's the bad news. But what's the good news? The good news is that in the same way that there is an answer for sin's temptation, there is also an answer for the effects of the fall that manifest in human sickness and affliction. This does not mean that Epaphroditus was sick because of his own personal sin. No. Instead, we simply see that he was sick because no one lives on a fallen planet without exposure to the effects of the curse, and included in the effects of sin and the curse are sickness, pain, and disease.

But let's follow this through. Paul hastens to add that Epaphroditus was made well through the mercies of God. And the message of hope and faith is that, like Epaphroditus, you and I may encounter sickness as we seek to fulfill our own life and ministry assignments; but if we do, the same healing mercies that made him well are available to us too!

Suffering while living in a doomed world is a challenge. As Paul wrote to the Roman church (Rom. 8:18–25), even the earth groans and we groan with it, waiting for that glorious day of liberty when Christ shall set us finally free at His appearing. But we are not to interpret the word "groan" to mean that this suffering has thereby conceded to defeat.

Never! The believer who endures life on a suffering planet can lay hold of God's promises. Read those verses and see the consolation that follows in Romans 8:26–28. From within the experience of our suffering, as we deal with all the realities of sin's effects, the Spirit of God empowers us with our faith to live victoriously, overcoming in all we do, and extending that life of victory to everyone among whom the Lord has placed us.

 FAITH ALIVE

Write out your personal philosophy for suffering in the three dimensions we have discussed: (1) persecution, (2) dealing with sin, and (3) living on a fallen planet.

1. Persecution:

2. Dealing with sin:

3. Life on a fallen planet:

Lesson 7/Saving Faith

When I was nine years old, our family lived where my dad was pastoring a small church in Akron, Ohio. I remember that time most, because that's when and where I experienced saving faith in Jesus Christ.

We were coming home from attending a meeting at another church. As we drove, I remember sitting in the front seat between Mom and Dad, and asking them the question, "Would you pray with me tonight to receive the Lord Jesus?"

They weren't expecting the question—not right then. I remember being surprised at how long it took Dad to respond. Finally, I heard him reply that they would pray with me just before going to bed. I vaguely remember brushing my teeth and putting my pajamas on as quickly as possible. But what I remember with absolute clarity is kneeling beside the bunk beds my younger brother Jim and I slept in. For some reason, I remember Jim peering down from the top bunk, probably wanting to see if something special would happen to his brother!

Mom sat on the bed and Dad knelt beside me, and putting his arm around me, Dad led me in a simple prayer as I asked Jesus to become my Savior and the Lord of my life.

I don't remember feeling a thing, but the moment is forever etched in my memory banks. Later, I would be glad that there was no rush of emotions. I don't remember anything of fear or guilt, no thoughts of heaven or hell. I honestly can't even remember what might have been said at the church service that would have prompted my request. But somehow, I realized it was time (I knew that I should!), and that it was possible for me to do so (I knew I could!).

That's what saving faith is. It's the moment someone knows they *ought* to receive Jesus, and that they *can* believe and receive Jesus.

Now, perhaps someone might ask, "Why do we want to study 'saving faith' in the context of studying an 'already-saved' believer's power faith? Haven't we been talking about *practical* faith, while *saving* faith has more to do with theology and doctrine?" But I want us to see how the basic faith exercised at our salvation is no different from that exercise of faith that accesses the power of God. Whatever it was you or I experienced when we *knew we should* and *knew we could* receive Jesus Christ as Savior and Lord, it's the same kind of faith we have been talking about!

Let's think it through: What is saving faith?

First, it is Christ-centered: *It is faith in God through the person of Jesus Christ.* The focus of saving faith is always towards Jesus *personally,* not towards Jesus as a mere idea. In other words, the moment you or I allow our study of God's Word to become separated from Jesus Himself, it becomes only an academic pursuit without the power of the Spirit teaching us and glorifying Jesus in us through the Word. However true the Scriptures are, and however wonderful their wisdom is, the *life* of the Scriptures is linked to Christ. We dare not separate the Word from the Person.

Read these following texts and write your observations in answering the question, Where did these disciples place their faith?

1. Acts 24:24

2. Galatians 3:26

3. Colossians 1:14

4. Colossians 2:5

Turn to the beginning of John's Gospel. As you read the first dozen verses, see how careful John is to present Jesus as the *Light* of the world, and as the *Creator* of the world. Now, see John 1:12. Note how the act of receiving Christ is made possible by the presence of faith.

What were those who believed and received given?

Turn to John 3, to the nighttime conversation Jesus had with Nicodemus. Here, the focus of faith is presented in the words so many Sunday school children have memorized. Read John 3:15–19, and write down the five times believing in the person of Jesus Christ are mentioned.

These and preceding passages make it clear: First, all vital matters center in the Person of Jesus Christ, not in "things," "ideas," or even "faith in faith." This is what separates living faith from formula faith or mind-science systems of belief. Second, *saving faith is awakened through the word of the gospel.*

Turn to and examine Romans 10:6–10 to help you answer these questions:

1. In what two places is the word of faith?

2. How is it heard?

3. What is done with the heart?

4. What is done with the mouth?

 KINGDOM EXTRA

Though the study on the language of faith is found in another lesson, something my father, Dr. Roy Hicks, Sr., has said might be helpful. In referring to Romans 10:9–10, he noted: "Here is the most foundational lesson in the importance and power of faith's confession found anywhere in the Bible. The principle is established at the very beginning of our life in Christ. Just as salvation (God's righteous working on our behalf) is appropriated by heart belief and spoken confession, so His continuing work in our lives is advanced by the same means.

The word "confess" (Greek *homologeo*) has the connotation of "a binding public declaration by which a legal relation is contractually established" (Kittel). Thus, as our words contract from *our* side the salvation God has fully provided from *His* by Christ's saving work and power, so we have a principle for all of life. Beginning in this spirit of *saving* faith, let us grow in *active* faith—believing in God's mighty power for all our needs, speaking with our lips what our hearts receive and believe of the many promises in His Word. Let us accept God's "contracts" for all our need by endowing them with our confessed belief just as when we were saved."[1]

Thus the parallel between "saving" faith and "power" faith is seen in its dependence upon the Word of the gospel.

Third, *saving faith is miraculous.*

1. Read John 6:44. Who can come to Jesus?

2. Read Ephesians 2:8, 9. What is the gift?

In this verse, there are three forces in motion: grace, faith, and salvation. Paul wants it clearly understood that under no circumstances can anyone ever say they were able to be saved by personal initiative. Though saving faith is your personal response which permits a gracious God to bring you to eternal life, this would be impossible without His free gift and His Spirit's graciously drawing you to the Savior.

 PROBING THE DEPTHS

As you grow in your Christian experience, this facet of God's grace—that is, that He is the initiator, the Author of your faith—will not only become more precious to you, but you will also discover that this fact about our saving faith has the power to ignite our practical application of power faith in daily living. Since God is the initiator, the believer has only to discover what God is initiating; that is, what does God's Word say He wants to do? What is the Holy Spirit prompting you to accept? When we have discovered the provision God has already set in motion, we may confidently appropriate it in faith, just as we did at our conversion when we received Christ.

Read Romans 3:21–26 and answer these questions:

1. Who has sinned?

2. How is the righteousness of God received?

3. Who is the one who is justified?

WORD WEALTH

Redemption, *apolutrosis* (*Strong's #629;* ap-ol-*oo*-tro-sis). A release secured by the payment of a ransom; deliverance, setting free. The word in secular Greek described a conqueror releasing prisoners, a master ransoming a slave, and redemption from an alien yoke. In the New Testament it designates deliverance through Christ from evil and the penalty of sin. The price paid to purchase that redemption was His shed blood.[2]

As you have answered these questions, you have reviewed and been confronted by the foundational principles of your salvation. It is a miracle, isn't it? Our salvation isn't a miracle because we were especially evil. You may or may not have been evil in the sense of being dedicated to the reprobate, depraved, or the terrible. But still you were lost—without hope (Eph. 2:12). Nothing you could do by any demonstration of human thought, strength, wisdom, or goodness in actions could rescue you.

But Jesus did. He rescued you! *Miraculously!!*

And why do I make such an issue of this miraculous aspect of your personal conversion? It is the normal tendency of human nature to forget the absolutely, overwhelmingly miraculous nature of this provision and power operating at the time of our experience of saving faith. With the passing of time, too easily does our personal conversion become a part of a scrap book, a diary of accounts, a memory of special times of long ago. However, if we can keep in view the miraculous nature of our "saving faith," we can keep prepared to experience many, many more of them—ongoing power moments of faith operating in life's *daily* circumstances just as our salvation did at our life's *decision* point!

But if we forget the simple, yet miraculous, nature of our original "saving faith"—how God drew us unto Himself, how He persuaded us, awakened faith through the Word—we'll become insensitive to how He is ready to deal with us today, and will be unprepared or slow to respond in faith.

Quite literally, every area of your life is presently intended to experience the initiating, drawing, winning, persuading work of God through His Word and His Spirit. Miraculously,

He is provoking you and me towards faith for ourselves, our marriage, our children, our business—every area of life.

Fourth, *saving faith does not rely on emotions.*

What is the antithesis to walking by faith? (2 Cor. 5:7)

Read 1 Corinthians 2:9–12.

In this passage, Paul quotes from the prophet Isaiah. His intention is to show that the relationship we have with God through Christ is not something that can be appreciated with the natural senses. Not the eye, not the ear, nor even the heart can perceive the things which God has prepared for us.

How can they be perceived? Paul says that these wonderful things can be seen only as they are revealed to us by God's Spirit. His Spirit does not show these prepared things to your physical eyes, ears, or to your heart, the seat of human emotions. Rather, God's Spirit reveals them to your human spirit.

Verse eleven specifically says that it is in our redeemed human spirit that God's Word and revelation can be received apart from the distortion which comes via the eyes, the ears, and the heart.

These are simple lessons that most believers learn early in their walk with Christ. You've heard it said and sung: "I am saved today, whether I feel like it or not!" Or, "I am saved today, regardless of what I look like, or what my circumstances look like!" And even though we may have learned these lessons long ago, *today's* dynamic faith life requires a review of those basic faith principles. Why? Because every promise we seek to apprehend will involve the test of our faith, and what Paul calls "the good fight of faith" (1 Tim. 6:12). Our faith will become strong only as we learn to trust His Word, walking beyond emotions—living and responding to circumstances by what we know to be true because of His Word, not by what we feel, see, or think on a natural plane.

Read Romans 4:13–25. Use these questions as you study Abraham's faith to help you understand what it means to walk by faith, and not by sight.

1. When is faith made void? (Rom. 4:14)

2. To whom is the promise made sure? (Rom. 4:16)

3. What does this mean to you?: Abraham . . . "contrary to hope, in hope believed. . . . (Rom. 4:18)

4. When are you weak in faith? (Rom. 4:19)

5. Conversely, and from the same verse, when are you strong in faith? (Rom. 4:19)

6. What would make us waver at the promise of God? (Rom. 4:20)

7. Of what did Abraham become fully convinced? (Rom. 4:21)

8. When did Abraham become strengthened in his faith? (Rom. 4:20)

Finally, *though saving faith is an experience rooted in space and time* (just as I clearly remember my experience as a nine-year-old), *it is ongoing.*

By this I mean to say, the faith you employ to trust God daily is that same faith you experienced when you first believed. Faith develops, faith grows stronger, faith evolves— *but it doesn't change its essence.* This is worthy and wonderful to observe and remember, because it points to how God is promising to meet every need in your life today—and to meet it through this same simple process of faith with which you began!

 FAITH ALIVE

Write out your personal experience of saving faith. Use words to describe how you came to believe in the Son of God. How did God draw you? How did you first hear the gospel, the saving word of grace? As you write of your experience, ask the Lord to show you how He has continued His work of initiating the possibility for faith in your life. Ask the Lord to show you any corrections, any repentance you need to offer, which will correctively address your life of faith so it can once again become saving faith!

1. *Spirit-Filled Life Bible* (Nashville, TN: Thomas Nelson Publishers, 1991), "Kingdom Dynamics: Rom. 10:9–10, Continuing in Faith As We Have Begun," 1704.
2. Ibid., 1692, "Word Wealth: Rom. 3:24, Redemption."

Lesson 8/The Language of Faith

Several years ago, I buried Nita Smith. I still miss her. Though she certainly did not have to work, she chose to help us in our accounting department at the church. Efficient, fast, smart, good humor—those are the words used by her companions at the office to describe Nita.

But that's not why I miss her. I miss Nita because she was one of those rare individuals who grasps the significance of faith in its application to daily life. Simply, Nita was a believer! She delighted in problems. Every negative was an opportunity for her to find a promise from God and put it into operation. With humor and anticipation, Nita would wait confidently to see what her faithful God would do this time!

I especially remember the Sunday morning she tripped going out the front door of the church. Since she had come to the early service, I wasn't told about her accident until the services were over. I rushed to the emergency room, but I was too late. She was already feeling fine, and in her words, "With his stripes I am healed."

As the nurses were finishing, I heard the humorous events that had transpired. When Nita fell, she hit her head on the concrete wall at the bottom of the steps. Like most head wounds, it bled profusely. One of the ushers called for an ambulance. This did not make Nita very happy. She wasn't nervous about going to the emergency ward, but in her view, it wasn't necessary.

The ambulance personnel put a temporary bandage on Nita's forehead to stop the bleeding until the doctor could stitch up the gash. Since her face was covered with the bandage, Nita took the opportunity to quietly speak praise to her Lord. But the attendant could see her mouth moving. Fearful that she might be in pain, he lifted the bandage and inquired if she was all right. With a twinkle in her eye, she replied, "I'm just praying, and if you'll leave me alone, I'll be able to finish before we get to the hospital!"

That was the first indication this little lady was not their usual Sunday-morning patient. Their second indication came when the nurse probing the wound thought she could detect more serious damage than just a cut. Nita's response was, "I've already prayed, and I know that the Lord has already healed me. If you'll take an x-ray, you'll discover it's just a flesh wound."

Since she had also hurt her knee, they took x-rays of it at the same time. The doctor came in with the preliminary report, saying that it did not look good. She had sustained serious damage to both her knee and her forehead.

Nita's calm response was, "But that can't be. You see, on the way here, I prayed, asking the Lord to heal me. His Word says that He will. Please take another x-ray."

Reluctantly they did. To their surprise, but not Nita's, they could find nothing wrong with her knee, and neither was there serious damage to her forehead. By the time I arrived, Nita was using the moment as another opportunity to share the love of her powerful Lord!

I lost count of the many times Nita would bring someone with insurmountable problems to church. She would smile through the entire morning worship, so expectant that God would heal, deliver, or do whatever her friend needed done.

I know she's quite happy where she is, but I do miss her!

I share Nita's story because, in this lesson, you will study several sections of Scripture which emphasize the importance of how faith speaks. Just as there is a certain sound to doubt and fear, there is also a clear sound to faith. People who believe, *sound* like they believe! They often speak a very distinct *language*—it *sounds* like faith.

 PROBING THE DEPTHS

Before you explore the rich subject of the language of faith, there are three major obstacles to consider.

First, *the language of faith is not an attempt to create a false reality.* Sometimes those who hear "faith" *spoken* think this is a kind of denial of reality. But this isn't so. For example, faith language does not deny the reality of sickness, nor any other fact of human fallenness or the earth's curse that has come upon mankind as a result of original sin. It is not a "pretend" language, as though we could take ourselves out of poverty, sickness, divorce, or any other reality which we may see or be experiencing. You can't, and real faith doesn't try that. No!

But there is a distinct way to respond to reality in faith. When you do, you will talk a certain way! Your language will employ words of faith. Instead of surrendering to the reality of the circumstance, faith will speak of what God's will is for the moment. Instead of dwelling on the reality's symptoms, faith will dwell upon God's promises. Instead of submitting to defeat or discouragement, faith will remember and praise God for His goodness.

Faith-talk does not practice the art of denial, but it *does* speak confidently of what God has promised to do *within* the reality we face.

Second, *the language of faith cannot be reduced to a matter of simply speaking positively.* Negative attitudes and language can be shown to be the cause of many failures, but speaking *positively* is *not* the same as speaking *"faith."* The language of faith speaks God's Word, whether it is positive or negative! Faith-talk employs the promises of God, not just the good intentions of man. Positive speaking has plenty of value, but the language of faith accesses the throne of God. The language of positive speaking may move people, but it does not move the hand of God.

Third, *even though this lesson seeks to identify the certain sound of faith, there is danger in thinking that once identified, this faith language can be practiced apart from an energizing work of the Holy Spirit.* (Please read that sentence two more times.) The Holy Spirit is the Spirit of *faith* and of *grace,* not "works." He gives living faith its dynamism. Nothing is more shallow than the appearance of faith without its Holy Spirit-given substance.

Think about this: one of the grave dangers to the life of faith is legalism. Legalism is the attempt of man to reduce the grace of God to behavior not requiring the energizing work of God's Spirit. Wherever Paul preached, those who were called the Judaizers persecuted him. His gravest concern was that the new believers would fall into the trap of what he called "a different gospel" (Gal. 1:6–9). Without the warm, loving, vital power of the Holy Spirit, even the truth of faith's power when spoken *faith-fully,* can become "another gospel" sinking into the dregs of religious tradition.

When it comes to the language of faith, every one of us needs a deep work of the Spirit, so that out of the abundance of our hearts, our mouths will speak words of faith (Matt. 12:34).

Read Proverbs 18:21 and answer these questions.

1. What is in the power of the tongue?

2. What does the tongue do which produces the fruit of death and life?

WORD WEALTH

Power, *yad* (*Strong's* #3027). Translated almost exclusively "hand," as "into your hand," indicating power, means, resource, and direction. The graphic aspect of the Hebrew language pictures the tongue with a hand! The tongue can, as it were, "grab hold" (as in this verse) of life and death. The words you and I use have the power to grasp or release matters of life and death. The phrase, "its fruit" (Prov. 18:21) indicates that the spoken word is also likened unto seed. Words planted by the power of speech become fruit-bearing plants, yielding either death or life, depending on what has been spoken.

Use a Bible concordance to help you do a study in the Book of Proverbs. Look up verses having to do with the tongue, mouth, lips, or speech. Here are a few to help you get started. Write out these verses, and your own observations on the power of speech.

1. Proverbs 6:2

Before contracts were written on paper, a binding legal agreement was a matter of words. What Scriptures could you use as a contract with God? What words would you speak to enter into that contract?

2. Proverbs 12:18

The spoken word promotes health. What words can you speak that would promote wholeness in relationships, in attitudes, in physical circumstances? What are some words that you have heard which do not promote health?

3. Proverbs 13:3, 21:23

Learning the language of faith includes learning what not to say. What have you heard yourself or someone else say that should not have been said?

4. Proverbs 15:4

From the margin of the *Spirit-Filled Life Bible,* an alternative rendering would be: "a healing tongue is a tree of life."

5. Proverbs 16:24

 KINGDOM EXTRA

Proverbs 16:24 reveals what God's wisdom (His Word) has taught our hearts: those truths and promises that are to influence our speech—to transmit that learning to our lips.

The Word in our hearts is to teach or control our speech and conduct. The "sweetness" and "health" such speech promotes are desirable, whether in our human relationships or in the release of divine grace in our daily living. It leads the believer to an overcoming, victorious life, through a consistent acknowledgment of the power and might of God with both mouth and manner.[1]

As you have studied some of the verses in the Book of Proverbs, you have discovered the connection God makes between the physical and spiritual world with your speech patterns as the gateway. Learning the power of speech is one of the basic lessons of the disciple.

Write out your thoughts as you review the following verses.

• The Word is spoken of as seed (Matt. 13:18–23). What can we do with it?

• The Word is also referred to as a "sword" (Eph. 6:17). In what ways may it be used?

• The Word is also used in connection with washing and water (Eph. 5:26). How may it be applied?

Having studied these references, how might they be given application in your life? Is it possible that in the same way God's Word is seed, your words might also be seeds? Is there a place for your words to be used in warfare? Or, again, can you speak words that have the effect of washing and cleansing? Of course, the answer is "yes." But this is only possible so far as you are willing to let God's Word become the pattern for your words. The language of faith is *speaking what God has said and what He is saying even now as His changeless response to present circumstances.*

One of the great teachings of Jesus in which He refers to the power of language is found in Mark 11:23–26. Read these verses before continuing, and write down your own observations.

Verse 23, concerning faith's possibilities and your speech.

Verse 24, concerning faith's release and your speech.

Verse 25, concerning faith's humility and your speech.

Verse 26, concerning faith's responsibility and your speech.

 KINGDOM EXTRA

Read Dr. Roy Hicks, Sr.'s, words on Mark 11:22–24, titled, *Jesus on "Faith's Confession."* "From Jesus' own lips we receive the most direct and practical instruction concerning our exercise of faith. Consider three points: (1) It is to be 'in God.' Faith that speaks is first faith that seeks. The Almighty One is the source and grounds of our faith and being. Faith only flows *to* Him because of the faithfulness that flows *from* Him. (2) Faith is not a trick performed with our lips, but a spoken expression that springs from the conviction of our hearts. The idea that faith's confession is a 'formula' for getting things from God is unbiblical. But the fact that the faith that is in our hearts is to be spoken, and thereby becomes active and effective toward specific results, is taught here by the Lord Jesus. (3) Jesus' words 'whatever things' apply this principle to every aspect of our lives. The only restrictions are a) that our faith be 'in God' our living Father and in alignment with His will and Word; and (b) that we 'believe'—not doubting in our hearts. Thus, 'speaking to the mountain' is not a vain or superstitious exercise or indulgence in humanistic mind-science, but instead becomes an applied release of God's creative word of promise."[2]

Because you are serious about your faith, and seek to learn the language of faith, you will want to pay special attention to the connection between speech that moves a mountain and faith that sends away sin. Just as we've seen, Jesus spoke of faith's language in both ways!

WORD WEALTH

In Mark 11:25, the one who has just been instructed on how to speak to mountainous obstacles is also taught in the ways of forgiveness. **To forgive,** *aphiemi* (*Strong's #863;* af-*ee*-ay-mee) "to send away." It is probably not a coincidence that the word Jesus used to describe "moving the mountain" is the Greek for forgiving sin! It is clear that you cannot send mountains away if you are unwilling to send away sins!

Holding a grudge is refusing to forgive, or "send away" the sin or action someone committed against you. The one who harbors a grudge will not be able to "move the mountain." You and I cannot properly address the obstacles in our path if we are maintaining obstacles (mountains of unforgiveness) in other people's paths. Forgive because you are forgiven. And in forgiving, you will discover even greater dimensions of God's forgiveness toward you. And your faith will be ready and active for mountain-moving situations.

KINGDOM EXTRA

"Believing can take opposite forms. It can be faith or it can be doubt. When you believe that God exists and that He loves you and wants to meet your needs, then your believing creates faith in your heart.

"On the other hand, doubt is just as real. The reverse of faith, doubt tells you that God is not real or that He is unloving or uncaring about your needs. Doubt gives rise to fear, which brings torment, not peace. Fear actually keeps you from receiving the good things God desires to send your way. Capture this truth: Doubt and do without; with faith believe, and receive. I have said for years, 'Expect a miracle!'

"Expectancy opens your life to God and puts you in a position to receive salvation, joy, health, financial supply, or peace of mind—everything good your heart longs for, and more!"[3]

Pat Robertson, answering the question, "How do I pray for a miracle?" said this: "When we are faced with a great need for ourselves, or for others, we should begin by humbly seeking to know God's will in the matter: 'Father, what do You want to do in this situation?' Jesus said, 'My Father has been working until now, and I have been working' (John 5:17). He listened to the voice of the Father, and He watched Him. Be careful not to start or end a prayer by saying blindly, 'If it be Your will.' Rather you should seek to *know* God's will in the situation and then base your prayer upon it. Praying for a miracle is welcoming a gift of the Holy Spirit to manifest. When His will is to work one, He will witness this to your heart. Then you can ask Him to perform the miracle that you know He wants to bring about.

"It is often important to exercise a key to the miraculous—the spoken word. God has given us authority over disease, demons, sickness, storms, and finances (Matt. 10:1; Luke 10:19). Often, we may keep asking God to act, when, in fact, He calls us to employ His authority by our action with divinely empowered speech. Then we may declare that authority in Jesus' name: we may command needed funds to come to us, command a storm to be stilled, command a demon to come out, command any affliction to leave, command a sickness to depart.

"Jesus said, 'Whoever says to this mountain, 'Be removed and be cast into the sea,' and does not doubt in his heart, but believes that those things he says will be done, he will have whatever he says' (Mark 11:23). Believe in your heart that it has already happened! With the anointing of faith that God gives you, speak it forth. But remember, miracles come by faith in God's present power, not by a ritual or formula of human works or willpower."[4]

Having meditated on Mark 11:23–26 with these remarkable teachers and leaders in faith's possibilities, take time now to write out your own thoughts on this key teaching of Jesus.

To finish our lesson on Language and Faith, study the words of Paul in 2 Corinthians 4:13. What verse from the Psalms is Paul quoting?

From 2 Corinthians 4:14, what does Paul say he knows?

Ultimately, your faith language depends on knowing the same thing that Paul knew. *It is the life of the Lord Jesus that makes sense of faith's confession.* Remember what Solomon said, "Death and life are in the power of the tongue" (Prov. 18:21). Because we know Jesus Christ is alive, and that as the Resurrected One He is ready to administer His mighty life-giving power to you—*now!*—in all of your present circumstances, we can choose to speak from the vantage point of life, not death. Our words of faith can confidently welcome and cooperate with God's will, as He has revealed it in His Word. We can enjoy the fruit of this language of faith—today and everyday— until Jesus comes again!

FAITH ALIVE

Write out a faith confession that has come to you during your study of God's Word on this topic. Also, write out a correction of something you have been allowing as an unbiblical confession that is inappropriate to your life of faith, and to your God-given potential use of the language of faith.

1. *Spirit-Filled Life Bible* (Nashville, TN: Thomas Nelson Publishers, 1991), "Kingdom Dynamics: Prov. 16:23, 24, Wise Words Bring Health," 905.

2. Ibid., 1492–3, "Kingdom Dynamics: Mark 11:22–24, Jesus on 'Faith's Confession.'"

3. Ibid., 1493, "Kingdom Dynamics: Mark 11:22–24, "Your Faith in God Is the Key to Your Receiving."

4. Ibid., 1999, "Spiritual Answers to Hard Questions."

Lesson 9/Faith and Restoration

What will God restore that has been lost? Is there anything God will not restore? How do I cooperate with God's plan to restore?

In this lesson, you will study (1) God's restoration promises and program of which we have historical record; (2) the biblical concepts of restoration; and (3) God's restoration promises for your life.

You will notice that I have placed this chapter late in our faith studies. Why? It is in our nature to study faith so we can accomplish our personal agenda. I am always grieved, and I think our Lord is too, when faith is sought out only for the meeting of personal need.

I recognize that this concern can be a trap. On the one hand, God wants to meet all of our needs (Matt. 6:33). On the other, God is actually up to something! He does not exist for the sole purpose of meeting our needs. From eternity, God has committed Himself to a course of action from which He has never swerved. In executing that eternal plan, He graciously meets our need. But the plan is much more than merely relieving the human condition.

Faith is at its best when you and I cooperate with God's eternal plan and join Him in His quest, instead of requiring Him to join us in ours! As we join in God's eternal purpose, we discover our needs being met while en route with Him to a final glory in which we have been included.

Restoration implies that something has been lost. No one can live on a fallen planet, deal with personal fallen nature, and face fallen nature in the lives of others, without suffering loss. Learning to live in faith will help you keep loss from regularly happening but it will still happen. When it does, because you have committed yourself to His agenda, you will experience the gracious and powerful restoring ministries of your God!

HISTORICAL EXAMPLES OF GOD'S RESTORING POWER

Zechariah and Haggai are two of the prophets belonging to the Restoration Period. The Restoration Period is generally understood to be that time after much of Israel's population was deported to Babylon. Israel was then repopulated by the Babylonians, and later the Persian empire. Even before the deportation began, after years of humiliating defeats at the hands of the Assyrians, God spoke through His prophets, indicating that Israel would be restored to her lands. As the Restoration began to occur just as God had promised, Zechariah and Haggai were used to remind the people of God's plan.

HAGGAI

Haggai prophesied during the efforts of Ezra and the people to rebuild Solomon's temple that had been demolished. The date of Haggai's ministry was approximately 520 B.C. and is recorded in the Old Testament book bearing his name.

The late Sam Middlebrook wrote of Haggai's ministry, "The Book of Haggai addresses three problems common to all people of all times, and gives three inspired solutions to those problems. The first problem is *disinterest* (1:1–15). The people had returned from exile for the stated purpose of rebuilding the temple in Jerusalem (Ezra 1:2–4) and had made a start on their assigned task; but opposition had appeared and the work had stopped. The people had become more concerned with building beautiful houses for themselves, perhaps in an attempt to blot out the memory of their exile in a strange land (1:4). To wake them from their apathetic attitude, God speaks twice to the people. They first need to realize that they are fruitless (1:5, 6) because they have turned from God's house to their own houses (1:7–9). All their efforts at building their own kingdom can never produce lasting results. After seeing their problem, the people then need to understand that God will accept what they do, that He will be glorified if they will only yield to Him what they have (1:8).

"The second problem is *discouragement* (2:1–9). Some of the older people in the band of returned exiles had seen Solomon's temple when they were children, so that no building, however beautiful, could compare with the glory of that former temple (2:3). The discouragement of the older people had quickly influenced the younger ones until, less than a month after the rebuilding began, work on the temple had ceased. But again Haggai brings a message designed to deal decisively with discouragement. The solution has two parts: one to deal with the immediate problem, the other to bring a long-range solution. For the present, it is enough for the people to "be strong . . . be strong . . . be strong . . . and work" (2:4). The other key to overcoming discouragement is for the builders to know that they are building for the day when God will so fill this house with His glory that it will surpass the glory of Solomon's temple (2:9).

"The final issue Haggai has to face is the problem of *dissatisfaction* (2:10–23). Now that the people are working, they expect an immediate reversal of all their years of inactivity. So the prophet comes with a question for the priests (2:12, 13) about clean and unclean things and their influence on one another. The response of the priests is that uncleanness is infectious while holiness is not. The application is obvious: Do not expect the work of three months to undo the neglect of sixteen years. The Lord's next word to the people is a surprise: '*But* from this day I will bless you' (2:19). The people needed to understand that God's blessings cannot be earned, but come as gracious gifts from a giving God. God has chosen Zerubbabel to be a sign (2:23), that is, to represent the servant nature to be fulfilled in Zerubbabel's greatest Son, Jesus. Note Zerubbabel's name in both the genealogical lists in the Gospels (Matt. 1; Luke 3), indicating that God's final, highest blessing is a Person, His Son Jesus Christ."[1]

Read Haggai's first prophecy in 1:2–11, and answer the following questions:

- The statement "Consider your ways," is used twice, and

brackets a description of their plight. How would you describe their condition in your words?

• Why did the Lord blow away what the people had brought home?

• The Lord has addressed sowing, eating and drinking, clothing, and wages. What does He say He will do about the forces of nature?

• In response to the prophet's first message, what did the people do?

• What did the Lord do that made it possible for the people to respond? (1:14)

 WORD WEALTH

Stirred, *'ur* (*Strong's* #5782; *'oor*). To arouse, awaken, stir up, excite, raise up; to incite; to arouse to action; to open one's eyes. Occurring about seventy-five times in the Old Testament, *'ur* is used of an eagle stirring up its nest (Deut. 32:11) and of a musical instrument being awakened or

warmed up for playing (Ps. 108:2). In Isaiah 50:4, the Lord
awakens the prophet each morning and "awakens" his ear to
hear God's message. See also Isaiah 51:9, which speaks of
the arm of the Lord being awakened or roused into action.
The present reference is similar: God wakes up the spirit of
Zerubbabel (and all the people) inciting him (them) to repair
God's temple.[2]

Read Haggai 2:4–9, and answer these questions:

1. In verse 2:4, the people are encouraged to be strong.
What promise does the Lord make for the restoration process?

2. What promise does the Lord make about the glory of
this latter temple (the one they were then building)?

3. From verse 2:7, how will the Lord accomplish this
glory of the latter temple?

You have been studying the prophet's word relating to
the historical event recorded in the Book of Ezra. It would
help your understanding of how God works in the program of
restoration if you were to read this book.

In Ezra 1:7–11, there is a curious noting of certain temple
artifacts. King Cyrus of Persia had ordered that these instruments which had been taken from Solomon's temple before its
destruction should then be returned with Ezra. The verses
even count out the number of knives!

Why is this partial inventory included in Scripture? Read
Jeremiah 27:21, 22. Approximately seventy years before, God
made a restoration promise concerning the articles of the

temple. "I will bring them up and restore them to this place." Why is this important? It indicates that whatever has been consecrated unto the Lord as His possession is just that! I've always thought it humorous to feel the Lord might have said, "And those knives, don't forget those knives. I want them back too. They're Mine!"

It's acceptable humor, but take great pleasure in this fact. Whatever you have consecrated unto the Lord—your life, your children—He treats as His and He will see to it that they are brought back!

ZECHARIAH

Zechariah's prophetic ministry addresses the same people but a different construction project. While Haggai's focus was on the temple, Zechariah's assignment had to do with the rebuilding of the walls and gates of Jerusalem. As the Book of Ezra gives the historical background for Haggai's prophetic ministry, the Book of Nehemiah does the same for Zechariah's prophecies.

The layout of the Book of Zechariah differs vastly from what you have just reviewed in Haggai. It contains a series of visions, their presentation to the people, and accompanying words of prophecy.

One of the prophecies having to do with the rebuilding of the city walls is found in Zechariah 4:6–10. Read it carefully to answer the following questions:

1. What will *not* bring about restoration or the rebuilding of the city walls?

2. What *will* bring about restoration?

3. What will happen to the mountain, the obstacle which seeks to prevent the restoration?

4. When the final stone, the capstone (which many think is something called the "amen stone," the stone that locks the arch into place!), is placed, what is being shouted? What does this mean to you?

 WORD WEALTH

The word **might** is translated "wealth," "valor" (courage), "virtue" (character), "an army." The issue here is dependence. What empowers your faith for the restoration you desire? As important as all these are in the program of restoration, you must not allow yourself to depend on human resources, courage, sheer numbers, or force. Ultimately, true restoration is impossible without God! The word *power* is almost exclusively a strength word and is translated so. As the Hebrew prophets and poets often do, this coupling of might and power is a literary and polemic tool. The one word is built upon by the other, so that when combined, a fuller picture can be seen. Here, the prophet insists that restoration is impossible by human might and power!

BIBLICAL CONCEPTS OF RESTORATION

The concept of biblical restoration begins with the Law. As an example, read Exodus 22. The first several verses deal with restoring something stolen, and the making of restitution.

WORD WEALTH

> **To make restitution,** *shalam* (*Strong's* #7999; shaw-*lam*). Figuratively, to be (or to make completed; by implication, to be friendly; by extension, to reciprocate (in various applications). Translated as "make amends," "finish," "full," "make good," "repay," "make restitution." It has the idea of returning something to its rightful owner, or making amends, in the sense of attempting to put things back the way they were.
>
> **To restore,** *shuwb* (*Strong's* #7725; shoob). To turn back (hence, away), literally or figuratively (not necessarily with the idea of return to the starting point). This word carries the notion of a fresh beginning. Going back to the start may be impossible in terms of time or geography. However, "restore" in this sense makes it possible to begin again.

If the Law calls for restitution that replaces with more than what was lost, it is logical to assume that the Lord who authored that law would do the same! This is exactly what you read in your study of His restoring the temple: He said that the glory of the latter house would be greater than the former. When He restores, He does something that makes the restored of higher quality than what was lost. In Zechariah 4:10, did you notice that the prophecy appears to rebuke the people for thinking that the rebuilt walls were to be despised as small?

Read Job 42:12. What does it say about the condition of Job at the end of his life compared to what his life was like before he experienced so much tragedy? Though Job is often used as the example of the one you wouldn't want to be like, the blessing of the Lord on this man who trusted Him through adversity is powerful.

In Isaiah 42:22, what is the condition of the people? As you read their circumstance of abuse, notice what the prophet says they are unable to do. They are so victimized that they are not able even to ask for restoration! Sadly, this is often true with those who have become victims. Whether real or perceived, the victim cannot conceive that it could ever be as it used to be, let alone think that it could be better.

Use your concordance and look up the references associated with the words restore, renew, rebuild, or build again. As you read these Bible passages, you will begin to see God's attitude towards restoring to you the things that have been lost.

This book of lessons deals with different subjects related to the life of faith. However, the book is not about those subjects; its about faith! The goal of this chapter has been to provoke your thinking by reviewing some of the historical illustrations of God's willingness to restore, and His methods to accomplish restoration. In the preceding section, you were asked to think about the basic restoration concepts. Now we come to the final section of our study in which we review restoration promises.

In thinking about this section, I have been drawn to many of those who will be reading this study guide, and who are asking restoration questions. If we were counseling together, and you asked the question, "How can I believe for my marriage to be restored?" or, "How can I believe for my emotions to be restored?" I would inevitably direct your attention to one, some, or all of these promises.

Why? Ultimately, restoration is possible only when you believe it's possible. Believing in the possibility of restoration is provoked by the Word of God.

AREN'T THERE SOME THINGS THAT CAN'T BE RESTORED?

Some might ask, "Is there anything that cannot be restored?" To that question, I would respond with the words of Jesus. Write out each of these verses in full:

Matthew 17:20:

Matthew 19:26:

Mark 10:27:

Luke 18:27:

Luke 1:37:

 WORD WEALTH

Although translated properly as it is, Luke 1:37 contains the Greek word, *rhema,* which means an utterance, or spoken word. In this setting, the angel has told Mary, "No Word God speaks is void of strength." Isaiah said something on this order, "So shall My word be that goes forth from My mouth; It shall not return unto Me void, But it shall accomplish what I please, And it shall prosper *in the thing* for which I sent it" (Is. 55:11). When you have a promise from God, you have the strength of God to bring that promise to pass.

RESTORATION PROMISES

In these promises, you will discover what God will restore. Though I have provided the verses, please read them in your Bible at the same time. If they are not already marked, mark them, perhaps by underlining key words or phrases. If the Lord should speak something of His restoration promise into your own circumstance, make a note of that thought in the space I have provided and make a note of it in your Bible, with the date.

The lost joy of salvation: Psalm 51:10–12—"Create in me a clean heart, O God; and renew a right spirit within me. Cast me not away from thy presence; and take not thy holy spirit from me. Restore unto me the joy of thy salvation; and uphold me *with thy* free spirit." (KJV)

This prayer of David is his response to the convicting work of the Holy Spirit following David's sin with Bathsheba.

It is included in the Scriptures because it models the possibility for the receiving of forgiveness and the restoration of the joy of salvation.

The lost sense of justice: Isaiah 1:26—"And I will restore thy judges as at the first, and thy counselors as at the beginning: afterward thou shalt be called, The city of righteousness, the faithful city." (KJV)

The thought here is that the ravages of sin have brought about an insensitivity to justice. A lawlessness rules without the honoring of absolutes, or the framework upon which a just community can be based. God promises to restore His people so their lives can be based on justice, which makes life available as it was intended to be lived.

The lost motivation for living: Isaiah 57:18—"I have seen his ways, and will heal him: I will lead him also, and restore comforts unto him and to his mourners." (KJV)

Read the verses preceding v. 18. What kind of attitude draws this promise of restoration from God? Notice the verse at the end of Isaiah 57. "No rest for the wicked" stands in contrast to the restoration of comfort and helps define what comfort means. It doesn't mean comfort in the sense of convenience. It has to do with no more mourning. God's restoring work will remove that peculiar kind of sadness that robs a person of his motivation for life. When the penitent one takes the steps to move beyond personal sadness or mourning and becomes contrite before the Lord, then the Lord will renew him in such a fashion that the ability to live again becomes possible.

Lost intimacy with God: Jeremiah 30:17—"For I will restore health unto thee, and I will heal thee of thy wounds, saith the LORD; because they called thee an Outcast, *saying,* This *is* Zion, whom no man seeketh after." (KJV)

This promise is special because it refers to an end of judgment. When the prophet Jeremiah spoke, "I know the thoughts that I think towards you, saith the LORD, thoughts of peace, and not of evil, to give you an expected end" (Jer 29:11), he was referring to the end of Israel's Dispersion; when they would be brought back to the land. The power of the Word is that it is spoken during the season when Israel is reaping the judgment she has sown. Even then, God is saying, "This will pass. This is not what I intend for you. I will bring you to peace. I will bring you to the expectations which are still possible because you are My people." The wounds in Jeremiah 30:17 are not the wounds caused by men. These are wounds received from the judgment of God! And so, to the one who has experienced the judgment of the Lord for sins he or she has committed, we can confidently give expression to the heart and will of God. He wants to heal the wounds of His judgment and restore your heart to Himself.

The lost time: Joel 2:25—"And I will restore to you the years that the locust hath eaten, the cankerworm, and the caterpillar, and the palmerworm, my great army which I sent among you." (KJV)

It would be enough if the Lord had promised to restore what had been ravaged by the plagues of locusts. Instead, He moved beyond the material substance, extending the promise of restoration to the time which had been lost because of the plagues! Sin and its consequences rob man of his most valuable possession: time. But when the heart returns to God, restoration of lost years in a marriage can be restored; lost years in parenting can be restored; the lost years of youth, when valuable lessons could have been learned, can be restored. Your years . . . can be restored!

The lost power to live strongly: Isaiah 40:31—"But they that wait upon the LORD shall renew *their* strength; they shall mount up with wings as eagles; they shall run, and not be weary; *and* they shall walk, and not faint." (KJV)

This restoration also has a condition. The renewing of strength is available only to those who wait upon the Lord. Use a concordance to see how this word is translated throughout the Psalms. The notion is that of dependency. The concept of being dependent on someone else is not popular in our culture! It is thought to be a sign of weakness, of dysfunctionality. But in matters of your relationship with the Lord, dependence is a strength factor. Your strength depends upon your weakness! In fact, isn't that what the Apostle Paul said? "When I am weak, then I am strong!" (2 Cor. 12:10). Also look up in your concordance how the word "renew" is translated. You will discover it has to do with change; renewing in the sense of something passing away, and the new taking its place.

The lost youthfulness in life: Psalm 103:5—"Who satisfieth thy mouth with good *things; so that* thy youth is renewed like the eagle's." (KJV)

The idea here is that regardless of age, God's restoring work will help you stay young. The eagle is referenced because of the molting, the process of replenishing its feathers. It may sound humorous, but eagles can't fly without feathers. They may have the muscles, the innate skill, and the opportunity, but without feathers, no high flying! Some Christians are like eagles without feathers! They have the muscles (the strength of purpose), the skill (they know the scriptural principles), and they have the opportunity, but they don't fly. Only when they let God satisfy their appetite with the good things of His Word, and allow Him to renew their youthful outlook, only then can they fly!

 FAITH ALIVE

Now that you have begun your study on Faith and Restoration, write out what you are trusting God to restore in your life and in the lives of those you love.

1. *Spirit-Filled Life Bible* (Nashville, TN: Thomas Nelson Publishers, 1991), Introduction to Haggai, 1356–1357.
2. Ibid., 1359, "Word Wealth: Haggai 1:14, stirred."

Lesson 10/Faith and Prosperity

The bike was red and black. I saw the note pinned to the handlebars. The same person who had left the bike on our back porch had left me a note: "The Lord wants you to have this bike. Because you gave, He has given to you."

As a ten-year-old, I didn't know much about "faith and prosperity." I'm not sure that I even connected the shiny new bike to the missionary offering I had participated in so many months ago. As a family, we had attended a special missions rally in another church. At the end of the service, the speaker asked us all to bow our heads. He prayed, asking the Lord to speak to us about giving to worldwide evangelism through our foreign-missions program. I was only ten and had saved some money toward a new bike.

Suddenly, I knew that I wanted to give that money to the Lord for missions. While everyone else was praying, I asked my dad if I could. He quizzed me a little and decided to permit it. I'm so glad he did! Dad put the money into my hand so I could place it in the offering. As the plate passed, I added my offering to what others had given.

It just seemed to be the right thing to do. I suppose others might have thought of it as a sacrifice. As a ten-year-old, I wasn't thinking so much of giving up my bike. Instead, I was thinking more of the thrill of hearing the Lord speak to me. It was the first time I had ever heard thoughts that were different enough from my own thought patterns to be arresting—to prompt the personal response I'd made.

No one had to explain it to me. I knew God wasn't *ordering* me to give—He was *asking* me to give. Somehow, I knew it was my money, my choice—to give or not to give.

Since then, the lessons of faith and the way they relate to God's promises to prosper His children, have been a valuable part of my life. I wish I could say that I've always been as responsive as I was as a ten-year-old! As I have grown older, the lessons of generosity have had to be relearned a number of times!

Let's join in this lesson to review what the Bible actually teaches about prosperity. Some promises of blessing appear to have little restriction. Others are very focused, with definite parameters. But above all, you will discover that we serve a generous God! It is in His very character to be liberal with His children. You will also discover that the conditions for blessing and prosperity almost always lead the believer down the pathway of *relationships*. In other words, though you will study rich principles of prosperity, you'll find that God is not interested in making anyone wealthy for the sake of mere wealth.

To secure a healthy perspective on this sometimes distorted subject of faith and prosperity, let's establish three things for a starting place.

CONDITIONS FOR PROSPERITY

1. Prosperity is always linked to **purpose.** God intends for us to be instruments of resource. Read Philippians 4:19: "And my God shall supply all your need according to His riches in glory by Christ Jesus." When reading this promise in its context, the connection between the Philippians's responsible actions of giving and the purpose of God's blessing is clear. They had given to Paul, and now God was rewarding them. But He was rewarding them so they could continue to be a resource for God's kingdom agenda.

2. Blessing is always connected to issues of **character,** God's and yours. Read Philippians 4:11–13. Almost in the same breath as Paul conveys the promise of blessings to those who have given, he is also administering the lessons of contentment. *Prosperity is never promised as a medicine for discontent.* Paul's confession is simple: I am content with or without. Possessions or prosperity are never to determine our contentment. This character issue is resolved by what one possesses on

the inside, not on the outside. It is in the midst of this point that Paul makes this famous statement, "I can do all things through Christ which strengtheneth me." It is clear from the context that this strength from the Lord Jesus of which Paul boasts has to do with contentment in spite of the presence or absence of abundance!

3. Success has more to do with God's **agenda** than with our **desires.** It is *never wrong* for us to present our petitions—our desires—before the Lord. It *is wrong* to make our desires a condition of our relationship. God wants to bless us, to grant us good success in every area of our lives. But we will discover that those blessings come more quickly to those who are committed to God's agenda for their life.

The Bible contains both *promises for* prosperity and *warnings about* prosperity! Why? Because the Lord knows our hearts. Fallen man—even the Lord's redeemed—is easily trapped into patterns of thought regarding prosperity that lean toward greed and avarice. The Lord intends prosperity to be a blessing, not a curse. But when greed is the motive, when prosperity becomes the condition upon which our faith is based, then our faith becomes misdirected. Suddenly, we are trusting Him **for** things, instead of simply trusting Him **in** all things. And that's when prosperity becomes a curse!

   WORD WEALTH

Prosper, 3 John 2—"Beloved, I pray that you may prosper in all things and be in health, just as your soul prospers." This word, *euodoo* (*Strong's #2137;* yoo-od-*o*-o) comes from the Greek words for "good" and "road." Thus it denotes success in reaching a goal, as in travel or in business.

Write out your thoughts on Third John 2.

John makes sure that the concept of prosperity is holistic. He ties together the condition of the inner person to the outer affairs of life. It would be unthinkable in his view to pray that you would get where you're going without being right on the inside. This prayer might be rephrased, "I pray that you will get where you want to go on the *outside* as long as you are getting where God wants you to go on the *inside!*"

 WORD WEALTH

Joshua 1:8—"This Book of the Law shall not depart from your mouth, but you shall meditate on it day and night, that you may observe to do according to all that is written in it. For then you will make your way prosperous, and then you will have good success." **Prosperous,** *tsalach,* (*Strong's* #6743; tsaw-*lakh*); to push forward, in various senses; to break out, go over, be profitable.

In the light of the Hebrew meaning of "prosperous," elaborate on Joshua 1:8, writing out your thoughts as to how this promise may apply to you.

These words spoken to Joshua as he was about to lead the children of Israel into the Promised Land underline the importance of God's Word in matters of faith and prosperity. *Tsalach* (prosperous) also carries the connotation of force. In fact, this word is often associated in the Old Testament with the coming upon a person of the Spirit of the Lord (see Judges 14:6 and 19 regarding Samson). In order for the new land to be occupied, there would have to be a breaking forth of God's power to assist Joshua. The word sometimes translated "prosper" is also used to describe how the Lord came mightily upon Samson during several of his mighty deeds of strength. It is as though the Lord were saying to Joshua, "I will come upon you and this people mightily for the taking of this Land, if . . .

Then, immediately following, this display of power associated with prosperity was conditioned upon speaking, meditating, and observing God's Law or the Word of the Lord.

It is no less true today. God's power flows fully through the lives of those who are willing to heed the Lords Word, to fill their minds with the Lord's Word, to give their lives to obey the Lord's Word.

PROSPERITY DEPENDS ON FAITH

Can you see the connection between the conditions for prosperity and faith? Does it make sense to you that not one of these conditions is possible without faith? Without faith could Joshua speak the Lord's Word in the face of all the obstacles he would encounter as he led Israel into the Promised Land? Wouldn't it take a living faith to fill your mind with God's Word instead of letting your mind be filled with the challenges of the conquest? This was why God repeatedly said to Joshua, "Be of good courage" (see Joshua 1:6, 7, 9).

How crucial bold faith is as we attempt to obey the Lord's Word! Try walking around Jericho seven times without faith! Try crossing the Jordan by asking the priests to enter the waters without faith. Read these stories in the first chapters of Joshua, and you will agree it was Joshua's faith, emboldened by God's promise of "breakthrough" prosperity, that triumphed. And how? By feeding on, thinking on, and speaking constantly . . . God's Word of truth!

It is faith, in these expressions of speech, thought, and action, centered in God's Word, that become the basis for God-given prosperity. Remember the definition of the word: prosperity—getting to a desired place. The idea focuses less on material abundance than it does on successful ventures. Godly prosperity is the heavenly provision which makes it possible for us to advance successfully on our assigned journey or task to be accomplished in His will.

With these thoughts, let's also remember how the concept of force is associated with prosperity that is a display of God's power and authority, never originating from human strength. I emphasize here: There *will* be resistance to your realizing God's prosperity. But God's power can overcome it and enable you to "get where God wants you to go!"

Write out your own thoughts as you study these verses dealing with the concepts of prosperity. Use a concordance to see what word is being translated as "prosperity," "prosperous," or "blessing." If there is an obvious condition which must be met in order for the promised prosperity to ensue, make a note of it.

1) Deuteronomy 29:9

Your thoughts:

Condition for prosperity:

Question: If the condition is met, is there any restriction on what might be prospered?

2) 1 Kings 2:3

Your thoughts:

Condition for prosperity:

Question: What language in the latter part of this verse promises Solomon success without restriction as long as the conditions are met?

3) 2 Chronicles 20:20–22

   Your thoughts:

   Condition for prosperity:

   Question: Since this promise for prosperity comes in the context of a battle, what did Judah do that made success possible?

4) 2 Chronicles 24:20

   Your thoughts:

   Condition for prosperity:

   Question: From the latter part of this verse, when does the Lord forsake His covenant people?

5) 2 Chronicles 26:5

   Your thoughts:

Condition for prosperity:

Question: Apparently, Uzziah had help in seeking the Lord. Who was his helper?

6) Psalm 1:1–3

Your thoughts:

Condition for prosperity:

 KINGDOM EXTRA

"Whatever he does shall prosper" (Ps. 1:3). This includes everything: your family, your children, your marriage, your business, your ministry, your job, and your health. It means God intends what He says: *everything shall prosper.*

However, no promise of God is without responsible action to be taken on our part. No one will prosper until he starts doing what God says. Many people want the promised results without responsible commitment, but none of us will ever gain anything truly worthwhile in just an instant.

The truly worthwhile takes time to develop. Do not expect God's answers to leap to *your* schedule. Remember, His answers occur when you first put His Word into action. Just as a period of intensive study precedes a college degree, so through patient pursuit of His promise may we wait for the Word of God to mature in our lives.[1]

7) Proverbs 28:13

Your thoughts:

Condition for prosperity:

Question: Since the meaning of the word "prosper" here is to be able to push forward, the confession of personal sin is the act which removes the obstacles that restrict forward progress. From 1 John 1:9, what does God do when you confess your sin?

8) Isaiah 55:11

Your thoughts:

Condition for prosperity:

    KINGDOM EXTRA

The editor of this study series, Dr. Jack W. Hayford, has commented on Isaiah 55:4 with these words: "Evangelism (the spreading of the Good News) and expansion (the enlarging of life's potential under God) both multiply by the 'seed' of God's Word. Jesus described the Word as 'seed' also (Luke 8:11), the source of all saving life and growth possibilities transmitted from the Father to mankind. All increase of life within His love comes by His Word, as human response gives place for His blessing. When received, God's word of promise will never be barren. The power in His Word will always fulfill the promise of His Word. We never need wonder how faith is developed or how fruitfulness is realized. Faith comes by 'hearing' God's Word (Rom. 10:17), that is, by receiving it wholeheartedly and humbly. Fruitfulness is the guaranteed by-product—whether for the salvation of a lost soul or the provision of a disciple's need—God's Word cannot be barren or fruitless: His own life-power is within it![2]

9) Psalms 68:6

Your thoughts:

Condition for prosperity:

Question: If the Father is promising prosperity to His children, what will happen to the rebellious?

10) Proverbs 10:22

Your thoughts:

Condition for prosperity:

WORD WEALTH

Sorrow (*Strong's* #6087), may have any of several different meanings: an earthen vessel; usually (painful) toil; also a pang (whether of body or mind): grievous, idol, labor, sorrow. When our blessing comes as a result of trusting in God, the blessing is free from the grief, labor, and sorrow that is associated with prosperity gotten solely from human endeavor. Most importantly, His blessing ensures that the prosperity will not become an idol! When God's people prosper because they walk in His ways, their heart's worship remains focused on the Provider, not the provision.

11) Malachi 3:10

Before your comments and analysis, first examine the two following paragraphs which give insight into this text.

WORD WEALTH

Room enough, *day,* (*Strong's* #1767; dye). Sufficient, enough, a large enough quantity, plenty, measureless. *Day* occurs about forty times in the Old Testament. Its first reference is in Exodus 36:5, which concerns a freewill offering of gold and other materials; the people gave so lavishly that the Scripture describes their gifts as much more than enough. *Day* appears in the title of the famous Passover song of thanks entitled *dayenu,* meaning, "it would be enough for us." Each verse lists a favor that God did for Israel at the Exodus, and concludes that, had He only done that much and no more, it would have been enough.[3]

KINGDOM EXTRA

Many people are handicapped by their own poverty, and too often their poverty is caused by their own disobedience to the Word. There are many ways in which people are disobedient; one way is in robbing God! This passage clearly tells us that those who withhold their tithes and offerings are robbing God. As a consequence, they are robbing themselves of the blessings that God wants to bestow upon them. You see, when you do not tithe, you are breaking the law; and if you are breaking the law, then the benevolent law of God cannot work on your behalf.

Nothing will keep a wise believer from tithing and giving, but he or she will never be found to tithe or give offerings just to get something in return. Rather, the act rises from obedience, and God *always* rewards obedience![4]

Now, comment on Malachi 3:10, with the preceding texts in mind.

Your thoughts:

Condition for prosperity:

OTHER CONDITIONS OF PROSPERITY

To conclude our study of prosperity and faith in a solid, biblical order, let us consider these three issues: Resource, Relativity, and Dependence

Resource. *Prosperity can happen only when God alone becomes the believer's resource.* Only then is it possible for us to avoid the poverty traps. The bank is not our resource; the government is not our resource; your monthly paycheck is not your resource. Most of the spiritual tests brought to the disciple's life focus on this key issue. Learning to look beyond the circumstances—to trust wholly in the One Who has promised to be your resource—is critical.

Read Philippians 1:19. Paul was writing from prison. Even though his circumstances were foreboding, he was confident that he would be better when this was over. On what was this confidence based? He knew that the believers in Philippi were praying for him. And he had immense confidence in the *supply* of the Spirit. This is what it means to see *God alone* as your resource.

 WORD WEALTH

Supply, *epichoregia* (*Strong's* #2024; ep-ee-khor-ayg-*ee*-ah). We get our word "choreographer" from this Greek word here translated, "supply." In modern times, a choreographer arranges a dance production, outlining the moves and steps of the dancers and performers on stage. In Paul's time, a choreographer was more like a modern producer. The ancient choreographer paid all the bills and made it possible for the show to go on! That's what Paul was saying. "I'm going to be saved out of this," or, "when this is all over, I'll be even a better believer than I am now!" Why? Because you're praying for me, and the Spirit is paying all the bills!

Paying the bills should be familiar to all of us. There are times when our personal resources, whether financial or emotional, are simply not enough to cover the bills. Paul recognized that his heavenly "Choreographer"—the One who is producing his life's events—will make sure that all the bills are paid.

Relativity. *God will always bless exceeding abundantly beyond what we have thought or asked* (Eph. 3:20). God's blessing is always linked to His purpose, *and* is also always connected in some way to the cultural norm in which his child finds himself or herself. The word "exceeding" is not the same word as excessive. In other words, "abundance," "blessing," or "supply" will always be relative to the culture. Let me illustrate.

God will not give a Rolls-Royce car to the rural Kenyan who has never seen a gas station. God will not give a million dollars to someone in a bartering culture. Yet, in every culture, His generosity *will* exceed our definitions, and even our needs;

just as when Jesus fed the multitude with the little boy's lunch; there were enough baskets of food left over to feed all the disciples. Having leftovers was certainly more than they expected, but it wasn't enough to start a supermarket specializing in fish and bread! Let us expect and contend for God's blessings upon our lives. Know that His generosity will exceed our norms, and yet not lead us to violate the cultural norms with ostentation or lavish display. His blessing is designed to focus people on the Blesser, not on the blessing.

Dependence. *Biblical prosperity is impossible without learning to depend totally upon God, and unlearning the skills of depending on self, or on blessings already received.* Read Psalm 30, the song David sings at the dedication of his house. In it, you will hear David confess that at one point he began to place his confidence in the prosperity the Lord had given him. This is far different from placing confidence in the One who gives the blessing.

"In my prosperity I said, 'I shall never be moved'" (Ps. 30:6). However, in the next phrasing you hear David saying that it is God who has made his mountain stand strong. Later in the Psalm, David speaks of his mourning turning to dancing. David was so blessed that, for a time, he placed his confidence in his wealth, his lands, his prosperity. (Though in another study we see that David's gross sin with Bathsheba took place during a time of unparalleled blessing.) But he later learned better.

Let David's life speak this important lesson into your life: When God has prospered you, it becomes even more urgent to lean totally upon Him. When you have prospered in your ways, it is possible for you to fall back into dependence on your prosperity, instead of continuing to look to the One Who has been the source of that prosperity.

Read Exodus 33:15. When it appears as though Moses might have a choice between entering the Promised Land with or without the Lord, Moses says, "If Your presence does not go *with us,* do not bring us up from here."

This choice of Moses stands as a beacon for every believer who learns the ways of a generous Lord. Be committed to His ways of blessing. Never choose the blessing over the Blesser!

FAITH ALIVE

You have read many, though not all, of the promises God's Word contains regarding prosperity. Write out a prayer which you can pray with confidence, asking God for resources to help you reach where you know He wants you to go in this season of your life.

1. *Spirit-Filled Life Bible* (Nashville, TN: Thomas Nelson Publishers, 1991), "Kingdom Dynamics: Ps. 1:1–3, Responsible Commitment in God's Prosperity Plan," 754.

2. Ibid., 1036, "Kingdom Dynamics: Is. 55:10, 11, God's Word, Evangelism, and Expansion."

3. Ibid., 1387, "Word Wealth: Mal. 3:10, Room Enough."

4. Ibid., 1387, "Kingdom Dynamics: Mal. 3:8–10, God's Prosperity Plan Includes Tithing."

Lesson 11/Faith and Prayer

Have you discovered the peace and joy that come from the act of prayer? I ask about peace and joy because I fear too many people want to discuss prayer for reasons other than *spiritual* benefits—too occupied with possible physical or financial improvements. It is natural, of course, for us to want to learn "secrets of success." Even when the disciples asked Jesus to teach them to pray, it might have been for the wrong reasons! (We know they asked unwisely for position and recognition—Mark 10:35–45.)

However, the power of prayer is found not in the assertive faith that seeks to require God to do whatever we may desire; but true spiritual power is in the aggressive faith which contends for (1) *the will of God to be done* (2) *as revealed in the Scriptures.* In order for this "holy aggression" to be released in a manner that does not become self-serving, it's crucial we become believers who are fully committed to the agenda of God's Kingdom alone—to His will and His rule. As that commitment becomes true of us, then the promise of Matthew 6:33 becomes truly available to us: "But seek first the kingdom of God and His righteousness, and all these things shall be added to you."

WORD WEALTH

Seek, *Zeteo.* (*Strong's #2212;* zee-*teh*-oh). In its good sense, this word means to seek—as in to worship—after God with all one's heart. In ancient times when the word was used with a negative connotation, it had the meaning of plotting or scheming. But when the believer seeks after God with the whole heart, strategizing for and welcoming God's Kingdom as an immediate reality—that's when the Lord can "add all these things" which have been desired from the depths of our hearts. Write out Psalm 37:4 as a companion reference to Matthew 6:33.

THE FOUNDATION FOR FAITH IN PRAYER

Peter called for a casting of every care upon the Lord (1 Peter 5:7).The basis for this act of prayer is founded in the knowledge of the Lord's love. That's the starting place—the foundation for praying in faith.

Do you know that the Lord cares for you? Only when we are convinced of the Lord's abiding affection for us—right at the intimate personal dimension of our lives—is it possible for us to come before Him in the simplicity of confident faith.

 WORD WEALTH

Care, *Merimna.* (*Strong's #3308; mer*-im-nah). A distraction, worry. This is the word Jesus uses to describe the cares of this life that choke out the seed of God's Word. It is the nagging thought that distracts you from the task at hand. It is the worrying thought that promotes disunity of purpose within, "a dividing, distracting, fractional thought." Perhaps this may be the best definition for worry.

 WORD WEALTH

Casting, *epirrhipto* (*Strong's #1977;* ep-ir-*hrip*-to). Actually, this word has to do with throwing or hurling, a graphic picture of tossing. Casting should not be thought of as a laying down of a care, but more the throwing away of a care.

Perhaps Peter understood how difficult it is to be rid of those cares; that is, that which divides the thought life. It may take something more demonstrative to cast away your cares than quiet, meditative thought!

Jesus knew the difficulty we would experience in seeking to rest in faith, believing that God cares about our needs. Read Matthew 7:7–11 and Luke 11:9–13. The enemy of our prayer life will often suggest that we will not get what we're asking for. You will hear his whisper, "Instead of getting your needs met, something worse will happen—and you deserve it!" But as you allow the truth of God's Word to shape your thinking, you will find yourself receiving Jesus' words; resting while believing that your loving Father will not answer your prayers with a rock, a snake, or a scorpion. Faith will rise in the confidence that God your Father—who has revealed Himself in the person of His Son Jesus Christ—will give *only good things* to His children; only blessing, not cursing, to those who pray to Him in faith.

A STRUCTURE FOR PRAYING IN FAITH

When the disciples asked Jesus to teach them how to pray, they had just finished watching Him pray (Luke 11:1). Do you suppose that they had witnessed something in His praying that was attractive?

In His answer, Jesus gives a very simple structure in which you and I may find complete confidence as a guide for faith-filled prayer. In the liturgy of the church, we often repeat the "Lord's Prayer," either in song, or in congregational response. Think through and then write your own "Lord's Prayer," following simple thoughts regarding Jesus' "Guide to Prayer."

• Our Father which art in heaven, hallowed be Thy name.

Begin with praise and worship to the Father.

• Thy kingdom come, Thy will be done, as in heaven, so on earth.

Commit yourself to His kingdom, to His agenda, to His will. Whatever you know to be His will for this circumstance, pray for it aggressively.

• Give us day by day our daily bread

Trust Him totally for daily provision.

• Forgive us our sins

Confess, and repent of every sin of which you are being convicted.

• For we also forgive everyone that is indebted to us.

Release every grudge; hold no punishing thoughts in your heart. Send away every offense committed against you. Release them from their sin to answer *only* to God, the righteous Judge.

• Lead us not into temptation, but deliver us from evil

Ask for grace to deal with any weakness of your life that might be prone to surrender to sin, and ask for His delivering power to liberate you from every bondage.

• For Thine is the kingdom, the power and the glory forever.

Conclude with praise over everything you have requested. Give Him all the glory.

Some powerful prayers have been written using this structure. Why don't you try to write one? Do not write with the thought that you will pen a prayer that will last a lifetime! Instead, write a prayer, following this structure, that is good for only one day!

As you do this over several days, you will discover your faith rising in a Father God who deserves your worship, whose kingdom commands your commitment, whose will is altogether good and righteous, whose daily provision is promised, whose loving heart has never condemned you in your sins, but has made a way for you to deal with those sins—whose love compels you to be as forgiving to others as He has been towards you. You will find faith rising in the One who will never lead you into temptation, but will lead you out of it!

Your version of the Lord's Prayer:

EXAMPLES OF FAITH IN PRAYING

Read the following verses and answer these questions. As you make personal observations, write them down.

1) Matthew 6:5–8
Where do hypocrites love to pray, and what is their reward?

Write your thoughts on the secret prayer and the open reward.

2) Matthew 26:41
What is the connection in this verse between prayer and temptation?

3) Mark 11:24

When does Jesus say you shall receive the things you have asked?

4) Luke 11: 5–8

In this parable, what appears to be the basis for answering prayer?

5) 1 Timothy 2:8

What Old Testament image comes to mind from this verse? What was to be true of the lifted hands?

6) James 5:15

Write out your thoughts on the connection between sickness and sin in this verse.

7) Matthew 18:19

 PROBING THE DEPTHS

As you study the context of Matthew 18:19, you will notice it is connected with matters of church discipline and correction. Yet the principle of two in agreement is an applicable principle not solely restricted to such matters. It's a kind of holy power that faith can release when Jesus' Name is invoked.

WORD WEALTH

Agree, *sumphoneo* (*Strong's #4856;* soom-fo-*neh*-o). To be harmonious, to be in one accord, to stipulate agreement. Our word, "symphony," is derived from this word. *Sumphoneo*—agree—does not imply that the availability of God's *power* is based upon *our* agreement. Rather, when believers are in agreement *about something that is God's will,* then this promised power flows directly from the Father.

8) John 14:11–14
Jesus gives the invitation, "Believe in Me," and follows it by promising that the disciples will do even greater works than He has done. Then He makes an extraordinary promise to them that would energize their praying. What connection is there between doing greater works and the prayer promise Jesus gives in verses 13 and 14?

9) John 15:7 (Study verses 1–7.)
As with the verses you just studied in John 14, these are also among the words spoken by our Lord the night he was betrayed by Judas. The "Last Supper" had just concluded. Many think that as they passed the gates of the temple, on which was engraved the emblem of Israel, the vine, that possibly in this setting Jesus revealed Himself as the Vine, and instructed their behavior as branches drawing life from Him.

Write out your thoughts on what it means "to abide." Look up *abide* in your concordance. Besides *you* being invited to abide in *Him,* what is promised to abide *in you* that will give you spiritual authority and fruitfulness in prayer?

10) John 16:23–24

This precious promise for praying in faith was given in the context of sorrow. What does the Lord promise that will replace that sorrow?

In whose name are the disciples instructed to pray?

PROBING THE DEPTHS

What does it mean to pray in Jesus' name? Today, as in the culture of the biblical languages, "praying in the name of" communicates the concept of representative authority. If someone came in the name of Caesar, it usually meant that they were an appointed envoy of Imperial Rome, with the authority to carry out a specific assignment. In legal affairs today, if someone is granted the "power of attorney," it means that they can execute a matter of business in someone else's name.

To pray in Jesus' name is not to use a mystical term that has magical power in itself. To pray in Jesus' name is not the license to use His authority to accomplish *your* personal objectives. Anyone today using a "power of attorney" in such a self-serving manner may eventually wind up in jail. In ancient Rome, anyone abusing the power of the Imperial court usually wound up dead!

By reason of God's gentle grace, nothing so drastic immediately happens to anyone abusing the power of Jesus' name. I've marveled at the mercy of the Lord in this respect, but I should remind you of the story in the Book of Acts. Some young men tried to cast out a demon "by Jesus whom Paul preached." The demonized man attacked them and tore their clothes off! Typically, people who attempt to misuse the name discover God's power is available for *God's* will, not *man's*.

In light of the above study, read James 4:3.
These people are praying, but not receiving. Why?

Write out James 1:6, then study the idea of "wavering" to grasp the meaning and significance of being *decisive* when we choose to believe.

 WORD WEALTH

Waver, *diakrino* (*Strong's #1252;* dee-ak-*ree*-no); to separate thoroughly, to withdraw from, or to discriminate or hesitate. This is a different word than the word "to judge," but both words contain the word, *krino.* On the one hand, we are exhorted to be discerning, while never doubting. We are to investigate a matter thoroughly, but once we have prayerfully committed the matter to God, we are to cease our examination!

Remember this: Once you have decided to pray, it means you have judged *(krino)* the matter to belong to God. To waver *(diakrino)* means that you now wonder if there is something else you are supposed to do, or if this is something God cannot, or will not, do. This is doubting. It wars against your faith and blocks the release of God's power from answering your prayer. Investigate the matter fully (anakrino); then make a judgment. If you present the matter to God in prayer, leave it there without doubting (diakrino—to think it through all over again!).

In light of the admonition of James 1:6, evaluate your thinking process. Do you hesitate (rethink)? Once you've given something to God, do you leave it there? If you struggle with doubting, what should you do? Write out your thoughts.

Having addressed your thoughts on doubting, review the story of Thomas's doubting in John 20:25–29. Take comfort in this: *Though Thomas has become a memorial to doubting, Jesus did make a special second trip to the disciples, just to reveal Himself to Thomas!* He won't forsake you or me, either!

FOUR PRAYERS YOU CAN PRAY IN FAITH!

1. The Prayer of Surrender.

A.   Jesus in Gethsemane

The greatest examples of this type of prayer are the words of Jesus in the Garden of Gethsemane. Read the accounts of this prayer in Matthew 26:36–42, Mark 14:32–36, and Luke 22:39–46. Not one of us can understand the agony Jesus was experiencing. Though we struggle against sin, we do not do so from the vantage point of purity as He did. We struggle to become pure, but Jesus was pure. He had never sinned (and never would)—it was not a part of His nature—and so He was in agony as He faced the potential of sin separating Him from the Father, as He was about to take our place in suffering for sin's penalty.

But think of it. Still, He surrendered! In Luke's account, an angel ministered strength to Him (Luke 22:43). Ultimately, He surrendered to the death of the cross. He was also raised up from the dead. Read Paul's reference to this in Philippians 2:9–11. In that same passage, where every believer is invited to emulate Jesus by letting "this mind be in you" which was in our Lord Jesus (Phil. 2:5), we conclude that if—as He did—we prayerfully surrender in faith to God's will, we also will be supernaturally strengthened, and ultimately exalted—with Christ as well.

B.   Mary at the Annunciation

Another great example of the prayer of surrender is found in the words of Mary. When hearing Gabriel's declaration, this young woman responded, "Be it unto me according to thy word." While the surrender of Jesus was based upon complete knowledge of what was going to occur to Him, Mary had no idea what would become of her commitment.

She could not know of the trip to Bethlehem; she could not have known of Herod's slaughter of the innocents. She would not have been able to conceive of being in exile in Egypt until Herod's death. Only later did she hear Simeon say, "A sword shall pierce your own heart also" (a reference to the death of Jesus), yet she said, "Be it unto me according to thy word."

Thoughtfully combine these two instances of "the prayer of surrender." There are some things you know about your circumstances and some things you know about God's plan for your life. With confidence, surrender to Him, to His will, and to His ways.

But there are also some future events of which you have no knowledge. Still, you will surrender, knowing this decision will possibly carry you to your own Bethlehem, to violent struggles with forces like Herod, or perhaps even to what appears to be a "detour" to Egypt.

Nonetheless, be like Mary. Reckon God's promise to be true. Know that His power will overshadow you too, and that something of His life and power is being born in you—His likeness is being begotten in you increasingly. Knowing these truths, say with confidence, "Be it unto me according to Your Word."

Write out a prayer of surrender that is significant for your life.

2. The Prayer for Deliverance

Sometimes, prayer has the sound of authority. The voice is raised, not to God, but against the enemy of the soul. As Pat Robertson has said, "It is often important to exercise a key to the miraculous—the spoken word. God has given us authority over disease, demons, sickness, storms, and finances (Matt 10:1; Luke 10:19). Often, we may keep asking God to act, when, in fact, He calls us to employ His authority by our action with divinely empowered speech. Then we may declare that authority in Jesus' name: we may command needed funds to come to us, command a storm to be stilled, command a demon to come out, command any affliction to leave, command a sickness to depart.

"Jesus said, 'Whoever says to this mountain, "Be removed and be cast into the sea," and does not doubt in his heart, but believes that those things he says will be done, he will have whatever he says' (Mark 11:23). Believe in your heart that it has already happened! With the anointing of faith that God gives you, speak it forth. But remember, miracles come by faith in God's present power, not by a ritual or formula of human works or willpower."[1]

Write out a prayer for deliverance that you can pray in faith.

3. The Prayer for Healing

 KINGDOM EXTRA

Read James 5:14–15. Just as Exodus 15:26 is called the Old Testament Divine Healing Covenant, James 5:13–18

is viewed as the New Testament Divine Healing Covenant. The inspired apostle affirms that those sick persons whom the elders of the church anoint with oil, and for whom they pray will be healed.[2]

"The Lord will raise him up" (James 5:15). That's the promise. What part do you play? If you are sick, call for the elders. Ask for prayer. Some have suggested that James refers to the prayer of faith as a specific application for this moment of healing. It is thought that in this instance, it is the elders who pray the prayer of faith. However, in a situation where no elders are available, you may pray the prayer of faith.

Write out a prayer of faith for healing or dealing with sin.

4. The Prayer for Revelation

Read Ephesians 1:15–17. With confidence, you can pray for "revelation." Because this word is being misused in some sections of the church, you may struggle with the idea. But Paul still accurately models for all believers a prayer that can be prayed in faith.

Perhaps it might help you to hear Jack Hayford's comment. In this text, Paul says he prays for people to receive "the spirit of wisdom and revelation," with the dual objective of their knowing Christ and understanding God's purpose and power in their lives. Such 'revelation' refers to an unveiling of our hearts that we may receive insight into the *way* God's Word is intended to work in our lives. It may be used of teaching or preaching that is especially anointed in helping people see the glory of Christ and

His purpose and power for them. But in making such a biblical use of the term as it appears here in Ephesians 1, it is wise to understand its alternate and grander use.

"The word 'revelation' is used in two ways in the Bible. It is important to distinguish them, not only to avoid confusion in studying the Word of God, but to assure the avoidance of a destructive detour into humanistic ideas and hopeless error. The Holy Scriptures are called 'the revealed Word of God.' The Bible declares that God's "law" (Deut. 29:29) and the "prophets" (Amos 3:7) are the result of His revealing work, essentially describing the whole of the Old Testament as "*revealed.*" In the New Testament this word is used of writings as well (Rom. 16:25; Eph. 3:3; Rev. 1:1)—writings that became part of the closed canon of the Holy Scriptures.

"Wisdom and understanding, as well as sound, practical speech, recommend that today's believer both know and clearly express what is meant when he or she speaks of "revelations." The Holy Spirit does indeed give us *revelation,* as this text teaches. But such prophetic insight into the Word should never be considered as equal to the actual giving of the Holy Scriptures. As helpful as insight into God's Word may be, the finality of the *whole* of the revelation of God's Holy Word is the only sure ground for building our lives."[3]

Write out your own prayer asking for revelation.

 FAITH ALIVE

Finally, faith and prayer are ultimately tools used personally and, most often, privately. Write out your prayer schedule for the next month. Taking what you have learned, what adjustments will you make in your prayer style? What corrections will you make to accomplish your goal to pray faithfully and in faith?

1. *Spirit-Filled Life Bible* (Nashville, TN: Thomas Nelson Publishers, 1991), "Spiritual Answers to Hard Questions," 1999.

2. Ibid., 1901, "Kingdom Dynamics: James 5:13–18 The New Testament Divine Healing Covenant."

3. Ibid., 1788, "Kingdom Dynamics: Ephesians 1:17–19 The Spirit of Revelation."

Lesson 12/The Father of Faith

My fondest childhood memories are about journeys. We took trips to either Grandma's house every holiday season. Thanksgiving or Christmas would find us loading the car to head for Colorado or Tennessee. The back seat would be loaded with suitcases forming a level area to serve as a bed for my brother and me. We thought it was fantastic. I didn't know until later that it substituted for a motel stop, and was based more on economics than on giving us boys some fun!

I suspect that with the passing of years, some of the fondest memories for you will be your journeys of faith. When Peter writes to the pilgrims in his first epistle (1 Pet. 1:1), he is addressing all of us who have embraced the Lord Jesus in faith as our Savior. You are a pilgrim—a traveler. Your journey of faith has many models in both the Old and New Testaments. Though all are insightful, none is as helpful as the life of Abraham. This lesson studies his life and his journey of faith.

I want to conclude our lessons on faith with Abraham for two reasons. First, Abraham, as the "father of faith," was given as a wonderful role model for the life of faith. Abraham was not perfect. He made some mistakes, but his faith began the covenant relationship between God and mankind which Jesus has now made available to all of us.

On a personal note, however, I want to conclude with the thought of Abraham because I have two models—two fathers in faith. One is Abraham; the other is my dad. Perhaps you've noticed I've quoted my dad often in these lessons. Actually, I've been quoting him my entire life, and at age fifty continue to be so very grateful for the way he has modeled the life of faith for me.

Second, I thought we should end by talking about Abraham and the fantastic journey of faith he took because that's what you and I are on—a fantastic faith journey!

ABRAHAM: THE FATHER OF FAITH

The Bible calls Abraham the "father of faith" (Rom. 4:11), and the father of those of us who believe. He is the one to whom God made the promise, "You will be the father of many nations" (Gen. 17:4), and when Paul writes to the Galatians, he makes the point that *everyone* who believes in Jesus Christ has become an offspring of Abraham (Gal. 3:29). As persons of faith, you and I have become members of the household of Abraham (Rom. 4:13), so promises spoken to Abraham's descendants are words that you and I can apply to our own lives of faith (Rom. 4:16; Gal. 3:16).

There are two sections of Scripture to study as we examine the power of Abraham's faith life. First, the historical narrative of his life began with the concluding genealogy in Genesis 11:27–32. Until God gave him the name Abraham, he was known as Abram (Gen. 17:5), and later the biblical narrative of Abraham's life concludes in Genesis 25:11.

The second section of scriptures dealing with Abraham's life, though referring to historical events, states a theological proposition. That section is found in Romans 4. Abraham is often referred to in the Gospels, and Paul also uses his life to effectively teach the Galatians. However, the most definitive section presenting Abraham's exemplary role in matters of faith occurs in Paul's Letter to the Romans.

THE JOURNEY OF FAITH

To follow Abraham's life is to trace a journey of faith that deserves to be seen as a model for every believer's "journey of faith." Read the following verses which list the major events that Abraham experienced on his journey of faith. Write your own thoughts when some particular aspect of Abraham's journey speaks to your own circumstances. How many parallel kinds of things do you see?

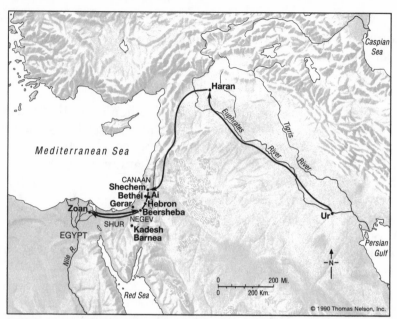

Abraham's Journey of Faith. Abraham's 1,500-mile journey was fueled by faith. "And he went out, not knowing where he was going. By faith he dwelt in the land of promise as *in* a foreign country, . . . for he waited for the city which has foundations, whose builder and maker is God" (Heb. 11:8–10).[1]

1. Abram leaves Haran for Canaan because of the Lord's word (Gen. 12:1–3).

The life of faith involves both (1) our response to a promise, and (2) our leaving of something behind. In Abram's case, he was called to a land as yet unidentified. While he had no idea where his response of faith would finally lead him, it was clear what he was leaving. The journey of faith is often like this. God makes clear only what we are to leave—to discontinue—while the future remains unclear. This doesn't suggest an uncertain future for those who walk by faith, it is merely unclear at times. Certainty is sustained by the Lord's presence and promise, even when we can't see tomorrow.

Abram's obedience in leaving is based on God's clear word of instruction, "Get out of your country, from your family" (Gen. 12:1). Though the Lord only promised to identify the land at some future point, His other promises were quite clear. These same clear promises may be rightly applied in the life of everyone who believes as Abraham did.

What six things did God promise to Abram? (Gen. 12:1–3)

1.

2.

3.

4.

5.

6.

In your journey of faith, perhaps the Lord has been just as clear and unclear with you! You may believe with certainty for the fulfillment of the promises given to Abraham in your own life if you are with certainty leaving those things which the Lord has clearly addressed. Remember the old saying of the church, "There can be no cleaving (unto the Lord) without leaving (the world)."

What is clear to you in your own journey?

What is yet unclear to you about your own journey?

What did Abram leave? (Gen. 12:1–3)

2. Abram leaves Canaan for Egypt because of a famine (Gen. 12:10).

Even though we believe God and follow His Word and way, we have no guarantee against famines! Our journey of faith—like Abraham's—will pass through famines. Such "dry spells" sometimes come in lost jobs, sickness, and/or other modes of suffering. Faith is not merely power to ward off evil. Faith is the God-given power to process reality. Faith never denies reality but moves through it in confidence towards God's promise of victory. Indeed, First John 5:4 specifically announces that faith is the victory that overcomes the world.

When do you win?

The moment you believe!

The fight of faith is not concluded in victory when you get what you were believing for. No! You win the moment you take a position of faith when you decide to put your trust in the Lord —in what He has said in the midst of threatening circumstances.

Some suggest that Abram should not have left the land God had just identified as the land that would be given unto him (Gen. 12:7–9). If this indeed were a failure in Abram's faith—if He failed to trust God in the face of difficult circumstances—it is all the more precious to note how the Lord dealt with his shortcoming. Instead of plaguing Abram for his lack of faith, God plagued the household of Pharaoh. While it does not appear that Abram was in a position to choose to leave Egypt, God intervened in such a way that Abram was provided for and virtually forced to return to the land which would become his.

Rejoice in this. Your journey of faith does not require you to be perfect. A believer is not someone who is faultless. However, a believer is someone who is responsive to God when his faults are discovered. Abram returned to the altar he had made when he first came to the land, and there he called again on the name of the Lord (Gen. 13:3–4).

1. Describe Abram's wealth when he left Egypt. (13:2)

2. Where did Abram go when he left Egypt? (13:3)

3. What did Abram do upon his return? (13:4)

Here is the lesson: *If you fail to trust God in the face of threatening circumstances, return as quickly as possible to the place where you first called upon Him, and renew your commitment.*

Write out any lesson you have learned from a momentary failure in faith. Remember Peter's failure? How did the Lord say He would pray for him? (Luke 22:32). Be sure to look up this verse, because this is exactly how the Lord Jesus will pray for you! (Heb. 7:24–26). And it is exactly how you and I should be praying for any we know who are experiencing difficulty on their faith journey!

3. Abram allows his nephew Lot to choose the better lands, and is blessed (Gen. 13).

This section reveals so much about the character of Abram! As a believer, he was not using human influence, personal authority, or advantaged position to contend for the better lands. He did not use his position of paternal authority to sway Lot. There was a total absence of manipulation on his part. Lot chose the watered land, the land that appeared to resemble the garden of the Lord. His choice left Abram with the land of Canaan. It was a large land but a land of deserts and mountains. Lot's land was hospitable. His choice of the best left Abram with land that appeared to be less suitable for the making of the "great nation" God promised.

It is interesting, even funny, that Canaan, which would not have been chosen by anyone, was the very land God wanted Abram to live in! Why? Because God intended miraculously to bless Abram, to cause prosperity to come within the boundaries of a land where such blessing would not normally have been possible! Lot's choice left Abram exactly where God wanted him: dependent upon God to fulfill His promises.

The lesson is simple: *When the choices of others leave you at a disadvantage, your God has you exactly where He wants you! In the very circumstance that appears to resemble a desert, He will fulfill all the promises He has made.* Sometimes our flesh wants to help God. It is not uncommon for sincere believers to make the mistake of manipulating their circumstances, of trying to "help" God. Though sincere, these efforts usually "help"—they help bring about the *opposite* results. It's a lesson that every man and woman of faith has to learn. For Abram, the lesson was taught early, and the Lord would like for all of us to learn this lesson as early as possible in our walk of faith in Him.

List any "desert places" in your own life which may have come about because of choices others have made. Then, list the promises you believe you have heard from the Lord and His Word, promises which you now know can be fulfilled in those "desert places."

Desert Places   **God's Promises**

4. Abram rescues Lot (Gen. 14:14–17).

Our study is about Abram, but it's worthwhile to size up Lot. His choice of the better land—self-centered in spirit—bore its bitter fruit. It brought him into association with Sodom and Gomorrah. Also, when the kings of the region went to war with one another, Lot became a victim of their struggle. Choosing the best in appearance without consulting with God inevitably will result in some kind of difficulty requiring you to be rescued!

In contrast to Lot's self-centeredness, notice Abram's generous spirit. When word was brought to Abram of Lot's captivity, he immediately gathered his servants and prepared to rescue his nephew. That he did so is yet another glimpse into the character of this "father of faith." The rescue was successful, and as a result of the victory, two important incidents took place that teach every sojourner in faith.

First, Abram met with Melchizedek. Melchizedek was the king of Salem, and furthermore the Bible refers to him as "the priest of God Most High" (Gen. 14:18). Abram displayed profound reverence toward Melchizedek, and offered him a tithe of all that had been taken in battle. Elsewhere in Scripture we are taught that Melchizedek is an antitype of Jesus Christ (Ps. 110:4; Heb. 7:1–10). When the "father of faith" paid tithes to the king of Salem, we learn that men and women of faith tithe of their spoils. We've discussed prosperity earlier, but make a note of this: *Believing people are generous in tithes and offerings.*

Second, not only are people of faith generous in tithes and offerings, they exhibit something else that is modeled in Abram's attitude towards the king of evil Sodom. Abram refused to allow this corrupt king to be a blessing to him. The king of Sodom wanted the persons taken in battle, offering the goods to Abram but wanting control of the people. Abram refused to enter into partnership with this king. Why? "Lest you should say, I have made Abram rich." God had already made Abram a wealthy man, and he understood clearly that his resource was a result of his relationship with the Most High.

The lesson: *A person of faith will not permit an association that will tarnish the source of blessing.* In this incident, our journey of faith teaches (1) rescuing even the not-so-innocent, (2) manifesting a generosity in tithes and offerings, and (3) maintaining a resistance to any partnership that would taint the source of our blessings.

Who are the people in your life whom you know you would be willing to rescue? List them, and be sure to include the ones who may not be "innocent"!

What is your personal "giving plan?" Evaluate your own generosity. If you struggle with the paying of tithes, write down the major reason(s). Also, write any lesson you've learned in generosity from your own journey of faith.

My giving plan:

My lessons in generosity:

Last, have you made any agreements which have tainted the source of your blessing as a person of faith? List them, and write out a corrective plan of action.

5. Abram's covenant-making sacrifice (Gen. 15).

When Abram complained that he had no heir, God promised that one born of his seed would be his heir. In this remarkable section, Abram was directed to look at the stars. As he saw the innumerable stars, he heard the Lord God say, "So shall your descendants be." Genesis 15:6 is extraordinary, and became a foundation stone for Paul's teaching on grace and faith in the New Testament. As Abram beheld the stars and heard God's promise, he believed the Lord. At that moment, Abram's faith made it possible for the Lord to "account" to him righteousness. What kind of faith was this? What does it mean to have the Lord account to you righteousness? It is having God—by His grace and choice in love—to attribute to our record the full complement of His righteousness and promised justification.

As you read the text, you will note that Abram hears the promise and believes in the Lord. As you become a person of faith, it will become increasingly important for you to recognize the distinction between believing in *the promise,* and believing in the *One who has made the promise.* For Abram, it was the latter that was true. And it was this faith that made it possible for the Lord God to account righteousness to him.

KINGDOM EXTRA

Do you struggle with the notion that it is important to put your faith in the Promiser—the Lord Himself—as opposed to only putting your faith in the promises? How I wish it were not necessary to even make the point, but it is! Why? Because you and I live in a dysfunctional world. Words are separated from context, making it possible to create new meanings for almost any word ever spoken. Words change in their meaning, sometimes drastically so. To make it even more complicated, as we've repeatedly noted, we are prone to take precious promises for our own agendas. That's why Abraham's experience in faith is so important. He *heard* a promise—he believed—*in the Lord.* See it, friend. Never allow the *promise* to be separated from the *One who has made the promise!* If you haven't memorized it, commit Second Corinthians 1:20 to memory: "For all the promises of God *in Him* are Yes, and *in him* Amen, to the glory of God through us." Listen to it again: The promises are yes and Amen—when? When they are *in Him.*

Read of Abraham's experience in Genesis 15:1–21 to prepare for the following lesson.

Paul later described this moment of Abraham's life seen in Genesis 15. In doing so, he used the legal and business concept of accounting. Hereby we see that God's "accounting" is a legal decision He made—and He is Judge of all. In this decision, the Judge justifies us as believers, giving us a position of righteousness before His judgment seat. Our faith in Him has moved Him to set aside our sins, giving us a position of sinlessness before Him. This grand moment of faith is realized in our lives as we hear "the word of promise" concerning Jesus Christ; when we choose to put our faith in Him. As we believe in the Lord Jesus Christ, Father God "accounts" us as *justified*—legally sinless, fully acceptable!

For Abram, the "accounting" was sealed by a sacrifice of blood. Abram prepared and offered the sacrifice, and then guarded the sacrifice through the night against the vultures. Sometime in that dark night, Abram experienced what is called "the cutting of the covenant." This term describes a ceremony which obligated two people to perform an oath or a contract. The sacrifice was laid out so that room for passing was open through the midst of it. The partners would walk through the sacrifice whose blood had been spilled, signifying that they were each obligated to perform the promise made on penalty of death. Amazingly, in Abram's sacrifice, it was God who manifested Himself as a smoking oven and a burning torch that passed through the sacrifice. Note: *Abram* does not pass through the sacrifice: *God alone obligated Himself* to perform the promise which had been given. Abram's part was to *believe:* God's part was to *perform*—to bring the promise to pass.

For us, the sacrifice is Jesus Christ. His blood has been spilled. And as was true for Abram, God alone has passed through the sacrifice of His Son, the Lord Jesus. Our part is to believe. God's part is to perform all His good promises to us which He has made in the person of Jesus Christ.

When we believe as Abram did, we are justified by the blood of the sacrifice, Jesus Christ. You have been accounted as "a righteous one"—without any sins, spotless before the Judge of all eternity! And it is not because we have believed God for *"things,"* but rather that in all things we have believed *God!*

Abram had to drive off the vultures, and similarly Jesus told the parable of the seed which portrayed the "fowls of the air" interfering with God-intended fruitfulness (Mark 4:4, 15). Write one example of how you have had to deal with the "vultures," the "fowls" that have attempted to interfere with the purpose of the One who has promised to save you:

6. Abram sires Ishmael by Hagar, Sarah's maid (Gen. 16).

Read Genesis 16, a story which presents Abraham's attempt to bring God's promise to pass without the Promiser! It was at Sarah's suggestion that Abram took Hagar as his concubine in order to have a son to whom could be given the inheritance. Sarah was barren. In that ancient time, barrenness was understood to be a curse. Her suggestion would have been totally acceptable in their culture, for her proposal was a common answer. But though understandable and acceptable within that culture, it is not acceptable for Abraham as a person called to faith in God. God's promises cannot be brought to pass through human strength or ingenuity. It is the Promiser whose miraculous strength is required to bring to pass the promises He has made.

Study this episode, paying special attention to the anguish that both Sarah and Hagar experienced. Note that God did turn His back on the results of this deed born of unbelief. But He revealed Himself to Hagar as the God who sees all, and He commited Himself to care for her and her child.

Most of us, though people of faith, have given birth to our own "Ishmaels"—to actions that beget problems when we tried to help God provide answers. But the same loving God who revealed Himself to Abram, who did not abandon the one to whom He had made such glorious promises, has not abandoned any of us, even though we may have attempted to bring His promises to pass in the strength of our own wisdom or might.

The name *Ishmael* means "God will hear." Even when we fail in a part of our faith journey, God will still hear! He does not leave us to the results of our fleshly thinking or actions; but he intervenes so the promise He has made can still come to pass in the manner He had intended!

What does the angel of the Lord ask Hagar? (Gen. 16:8)

What does angel of the Lord instruct Hagar to do? (Gen. 16:9)

What name does Hagar give to God? (Gen. 16:13)

7. Abram's name is changed to Abraham (Gen. 17).

Abram's name is changed to Abraham. Abram meant "high father," but Abraham means "father of many nations." At this moment, God institutes a sign of the covenant agreement.

Write out the covenant God made with Abraham. (Gen. 17:7)

What was the sign of the covenant?

What was the penalty if this sign of the covenant were not performed? (Gen. 17:14)

It is important to note that although Abraham offered many sacrifices during his journey of faith, there was only one sacrifice which was accounted to him for righteousness (Gen. 15). Remember that: many sacrifices involved worship and faith but only one served as the moment of saving faith. Though the lack of circumcision would cause the non-participant to be disenfranchised from the covenant, circumcision itself was not the moment of saving faith. It was the *sign* of the covenant, not the covenant itself.

In the New Testament, the Pharisees placed great value on outward holiness. During Paul's missionary journeys this same philosophy was promulgated by the Judaizers. In Paul's letter to the Philippians, he lists the signs of the new covenant. This new covenant is established in the blood sacrifice of Jesus Christ. Only one sacrifice is necessary to ensure your covenant with God. While the sign of Abraham's covenant was a physical surgery—a permanent mark on his body—your and my sign as people of the covenant is no less permanent. However, instead of being a mark on our bodies, we are marked by how we live before God and man.

What are the signs of the new covenant? (Phil. 3:1–3)

8. Abraham is promised a son through Sarah (Gen. 18:1–15).

In Genesis 18, the incident of Abraham's name change is recorded, along with an appearance of the Lord, accompanied by two angels. They are on their way to judge Sodom and Gomorrah when they stop to visit Abraham. As Abraham serves them with the traditional washing of the feet and the offering of food from his provisions, the Lord speaks to him.

What did Abraham do when he met the angels? (Gen. 18:3)

What was the response of Sarah when she overheard the conversation between Abraham and the angels? (Gen. 18:12)

What was Abraham's response? (Gen. 17:17)

How did God admonish Sarah? (Gen. 18:14)

How old were Abraham and Sarah at that time? (Gen. 17:17)

How old was Abraham when Ishmael was born? (Gen. 16:16)

 FAITH ALIVE

One of the great lessons to be learned from Abraham's journey of faith has to do with time. You and I live in a culture in which time has the appearance of being compressed. Most things can be done quickly, if not immediately. Faxes, computers, and microwaves all make for immediacy. However, faith does not operate in such an atmosphere of immediacy or convenience. At that point in Abraham's journey, God had promised him a son many years before. It may be that Abraham's laugh had less to do with unbelief, and more to do with the failure to understand God's promises in light of how God moves in time.

This is especially true for people whose concept of time and space has become distorted through technology. Faith can have immediate results. And sometimes, faith can even have convenient results! The mistake is to assume that in the passing of time, the promise has been set aside or that God has decided to permit His promise to be fulfilled through an Ishmael, through the results of human provision, rather than through His own miraculous power and timing. Write out the promises you know you have received from God's Word and God's Spirit, and which require your patience in faith.

9. Abraham's Call to Sacrifice Isaac (Gen. 22)

Finally, Abraham faced the supreme call to faith: to lay everything God had given him on the altar. To surrender even the fulfilled promise, and to trust the Promiser above all.

Read Genesis 22. Answer these questions.

1. How did God word His command to Abraham? (v. 2)

2. What time lapse intervened before Abraham responded? (v. 3)

3. What evidence did Abraham's words give that he believed God would intervene? (v. 5)

4. When questioned by Isaac, who sensed the unusual situation, what did Abraham answer? (vv. 6–8)

5. How far did Abraham proceed in his action of obedience? (vv. 9–10)

6. What did God say, do, and direct? (vv. 11–13)

7. Why did God say He was intervening? (v. 12)

Now, go back over each point and draw an applied lesson to your own life.

1.

2.

3.

4.

5.

6.

7.

This encounter was the essential climax of Abraham's life-long journey of faith. God's highest purposes are not to make us wealthy (though He did that with Abraham), to make us well (though He "healed" Abraham's body and enabled Isaac's birth), or to fulfill His promise to us (though He did give Abraham and Sarah their promised son, Isaac). His goal is to bring us to the place where we will trust Him on all terms, in every situation, and walk with Him—above and beyond all.

And this, fellow pilgrim, is the final truth that all of faith's lessons are intended to engrave upon our souls. Write a prayer that this lesson will sink into your own soul and abide with you forever.

A LAST WORD

We've finished our faith lessons. Or have we? Isn't it true that our journey of faith will not really be complete until we stand before our Father? I will rejoice if any exercise in this study guide on faith, or any words you have read from me or from those I have quoted, will help you on your personal faith journey.

Ultimately, when we stand before God, our faith is what will bring Him honor and glory. "That the genuineness of your faith, *being* much more precious than gold that perishes, though it is tested by fire, may be found to praise, honor, and glory at the revelation of Jesus Christ" (1 Pet. 1:7).

And our faith will be . . . tried with fire! The word picture in the Greek text is that of a goldsmith who repeatedly heats the ore, drawing off the "dross" (impurities, slag, waste) as it comes to the surface of the melted metal. When does the goldsmith know he is finished? We are told that in ancient times, the refiner knew he was finished with the purifying process only when he could clearly see his own reflection in the gold.

And in the same manner, our loving Lord Jesus will faithfully be our companion through every fiery trial. As we submit to life's dealings in His presence, as we confess our impurities that surface because of the heat of circumstances, He will lovingly remove all the "dross" from our lives. However far along in that process each of us moves, on one glorious day we will stand before Him. And as the last of the impurities will have been removed, we will see His image perfected: "We shall be like Him, for we shall see Him as He is" (1 John 3:2).

And so, my brother and sister, let us grow in faith and thereby grow in Christ: "May our faith, tested by fire, be found unto Him in all praise and honor and glory!" Amen.

> *He is able to keep you from falling,*
> *And to present you before His glorious throne.*
> *I shall appear without fault and with joy.*
> *For He is able,*
> *Yes, Jesus is able,*
> *To keep me from falling—He is able.*
>
> Roy Hicks, Jr.

(a song lyric drawn from Jude 24)

---

1. *Spirit-Filled Life Bible* (Nashville, TN: Thomas Nelson Publishers, 1991), "Abraham's Journey of Faith," 23.